Advancing Science with Dreams and Visions

Advancing Science with Dreams and Visions

John White

Copyright © 2023
All Rights Reserved

Dedication

I have been surrounded by some great people that helped make me become a person that could write this book and who deserves all my thanks.

John Wimber, along with other Vineyard leaders. By their example and by allowing me to be a partner with them, I apprehended the spirit-filled life and learned to be a constant worshipper. I saw the Kingdom where everyone "played."

Nick Gough, a longtime friend and pastor, encouraged me to seriously pursue spiritual gifts and especially revelatory gifts like prophecy and words of knowledge and wisdom. Your friendship is unequalled and means everything to me. We're almost there. It's all downhill. It's not that bad.

My family, who has seen my very best and my very worst yet still love me. I have learned so much from you all, but more importantly, you are my foundation that steady me when life can't be better and when it can't be worse. I am so grateful for the miles of smiles, laughter and for singing about magic dragons and red rhinoceroses.

Table of Contents

Dedication i
Reticule 1
Setting the Stage 4
Introduction 13
    Inspiration Insights 22
Science and Mystery 23
    Inspiration Insights 32
Inspiration 33
    Inspiration Insights 48
Testing and Proving 49
    Reputation 49
    Technology Marketplace Skepticism 53
    Relevance 54
    Confidence in hearing God's voice 57
    Morality 60
    Inspiration Insights 64
Translation and Communication 65
    Marketplace Language 66
    Collaboration 69
    God's Grace 70
    Inspiration Insights 71
Development and Evolution (Putting Flesh on Dry Bones) 73
    Inspiration insights 85

Qualification and Verification 86
    Inspiration Insights 89
Implementation 90
    Inspiration Insights 98
Tell the World 99
    Inspiration Insights 108
Remembrance and Memorials 110
Finale 113
About the Author 116
Acknowledgements 119

Reticule

Christian technologists and scientists face a similar evangelistic challenge as the apostle Paul faced when he preached at Mars Hill near Athens, Greece. Paul piqued the intellectuals' and philosophers' interest in the gospel by teaching in Athens's synagogues and marketplaces. They invited Paul to speak at the Areopagus. At Mars Hill, Paul made his appeal to the intellectual crowd. The result was only a few believed and followed Paul. The next city in Paul's mission was Corinth. Paul adjusted his tactics and described them, saying, "For the message of the cross is foolishness to those who are perishing, but to us who are being saved, it is the power of God (1 Corinthians 1:18)." It appears appealing to intellectualism and philosophy has little fruit while demonstrating the power of God has much fruit.

Spiritual gifts are explosive tools for evangelistic demonstrations of God's power and open doors to meaningful spiritual conversations in all marketplaces. However, if the demonstrations are copied as they are in our churches, they will mostly be irrelevant for the workplace environment. Further, many companies have human resource policies preventing religious displays and messaging. Therefore, the unsaved in the marketplace will likely ascribe supernatural phenomena to someone or something other than Jesus. I have prayed for and seen people healed from a physical infirmity in my office at work. If this happens at church, people applaud and thank God for a miraculous intervention. However, at work, the response is quite different. My teammates were not persuaded toward the message of the gospel even when they witnessed a healing miracle.

At the heart of this book is the understanding that God wants humanity to be saved and to advance in all areas, including humanity's understanding of their world in time and space. In church, we see the advancement of God's kingdom in salvation, disciple-making, binding or casting out demons, and spiritual formation, healing, and speaking in tongues, which according to 1 Corinthians 14, is a sign to the unbeliever, miracles, and revelation for specific life situations. This book suggests the same spiritual gifts of prophecy, knowledge, and wisdom discussed in 1 Corinthians 12 and 14 and Romans 12 and practiced in our churches can advance the Kingdom in the entire marketplace, including science and technology, and that these advancements are equally a testimony to the power and nature of God as healings or miracles are in church.

This book uses specific examples showing how divine revelation affected major engineering programs, including the International Space Station (ISS). It includes sections on how to translate a non-verbal revelation to the technology marketplace, an example of how to develop revelation within the scientific method, how to communicate revelation within the scientific and technology cultures, and how to manage development, communication within your workplace and associates, implementation and peer review.

While the examples are rooted in an aerospace environment, the intent is the reader from other marketplaces can apply the same principles and processes to advance medicine, engineering, computer science, transportation, architecture, energy, infrastructure, aerospace, and other important technology fields.

Christian technologists have an opportunity to lead technology breakthroughs through the revelatory gifts available to all Christians. It seems God is happy to help humanity understand the world around them. He is equally happy to exalt His children among their peers not only because of their integrity but also because of their ability to advance technology. Throughout this book is an evangelistic priority which includes a discussion on how technological advancements lead to evangelistic opportunities where apologetics fail.

Setting the Stage

A man's gift makes room for him and brings him before great men (Proverbs 18:16)[1]

In the last hundred years, the world has witnessed mind-boggling technical advancement; some may even call it miraculous. This technology explosion has significantly impacted nearly every aspect of our society. In 1954, Jacques Ellul, whom some call a 'Technology Prophet,' wrote, "Modern technology has become a total phenomenon for civilization, the defining force of a new social order in which efficiency is no longer an option but a necessity imposed on all human activity."[2] With the ever-increasing demand for technical advancement that Jacques Ellul predicted and which we are now experiencing, the internet has become rich in business articles on how to stimulate technology innovators within industry and government. Typical articles focus on improving and maximizing researchers', technologists', and scientists' productivity. The undermining consequences of

---

[1] The New King James Version. Nashville: Thomas Nelson ©1982. (Pr 18:16).
[2] Ellul, Jacques, "The Technical Society" Alfred A. Knopf Inc. and Random House, Toronto, © 1964 (English), © 1954 (French).

pushing for and demanding higher technical innovation productivity is fatigue and burnout, resulting in reduced overall productivity and, worse, reduced technical creativity. Among the many adverse effects of stress in the workplace is reduced creativity, according to Buisness.com. About the relationship between stress and reduced creativity, Business.com says, "Being stressed causes your mind to wander, preventing you from locking in on new ideas. It basically limits your ability to come up with creative, new ideas."[3]

These innovation productivity experts say little about how to keep technologists, scientists, and researchers inspired and innovative. It begs the question, "How are innovators inspired?" Of course, businesses wish to stimulate and expedite technology development and reduce development cycles to gain competitive advantages. Tech companies today can no longer afford to wait a lifetime to develop a theory or product.

Let's use the telephone as an example to illustrate the shortening of the technology development cycle. The first rotary phone was demonstrated in 1892 and was basically unchanged until 1963 when the push-button telephone was introduced. That is nearly seventy years! Today, the typical life

---

[3] Peak, Sean, "Stress and Productivity: What the Numbers Say," © 2023, https://www.business.com/articles/stress-and-productivity-what-the-numbers-say

cycle for a phone is two to three years. The next iterations include new operating systems, new physical and software features, new user interfaces, hardware upgrades, like cameras, and continuing miniaturization. Not only are technology development life cycles shortened, but the amount of new technology contained in each new device release increases exponentially. In 1965, Gordon Moore, the co-founder of Intel, observed the number of transistors on microchips doubles about every two years. This advancement, known as Moore's Law, applies not only to computer chips but nearly every other technology field.

Thomas Edison, a notable innovator and someone familiar with technology innovation and development, says, "Genius is one percent inspiration and ninety-nine percent perspiration." Schools teach technologists about the 99%. My engineering curriculum included calculus, differential equations, physics, thermodynamics, fluid dynamics, and strength of materials, among many others. The engineering curriculum gave me a set of tools allowing me to develop, analyze and prove different ideas. The same is true for most technologists who are taught similar sets of rules for their chosen technology fields, enabling them to evaluate the world with respect to their interests. Our educational institutions teach us the 99% portions of Edison's equation.

Most students entering Science, Technology, Engineering, and Mathematics (STEM) education expect they will gain the skills to invent and develop new technology and science. Nothing is farther from the truth. An uninspired person will not immerge from a STEM education more inspired than when they started. And contrary to what some think, inspiration rarely comes like lightning. The history of science innovation shows most changes in science and technology are neither quick nor concise. Further, innovations that advance science and technology are rarely specific to a workplace problem despite this being assumed in most magazine articles on the subject.

Technical innovation non-specificity can be illustrated in the process of disclosing patents. When I worked on the International Space Station (ISS), I had several dreams about on-orbit system maintenance. I dreamt astronauts were trying to perform certain space-walk tasks, getting frustrated because they did not have the correct tools. After several months of recurring dreams, I realized my dream life was telling me new tools were needed. I identified six or seven tools that no one ever considered before and, as such, were patentable. I also found that derivatives of the tool configurations that would facilitate terrestrial technicians, especially in hazardous work areas. At that time, my company was pushing engineers for new innovations and patents. I submitted multiple technology disclosures covering a few of the tools to the company's patent office. However, my company did not pursue the technology because the ISS contract did not include maintenance and on-orbit servicing. They decided the development was not specific enough to allow capitalization with respect to their current business opportunities. I was discouraged by that decision, and these submittals became the last I submitted to that company. Imagine how valuable technologists would be if they were 'rapid-fire' inspirationalists with a high ratio of technical inspiration conversion to technology advancements and new product development that the company could capitalize!

Let's talk about what it means to be a technology and science inspirationalist as distinguished from being a researcher and developer. Proverbs 25:2 says, "It is the glory of God to conceal a matter; to search out a matter is the glory of kings." Our world is full of mystery. People who advance science and technology embrace mystery and inspiration. The inspiration to advance technology is similar to an artist who wants to express an image they have never seen or a musician creating a new song or sound. At the core of technological innovation is revelation that seems intangible, having no form. Usually, revelation at the elemental level, what I call the kernel of inspiration, is often non-verbal, difficult to describe precisely, and involves a non-logical activation within the mind and spirit. These subjects are taboo in the academic and technology worlds and nearly so in the business world. The kernel of inspiration falls into the world of the mysterious and therefore is difficult to teach with a precise outcome. Specifically, how would you grade a student's technical kernel of inspiration if he lacks the tools to communicate what he senses as non-verbal? Mystery creates an education gap in the technology curriculum, especially since most STEM educators sneer at the irrational creative process typically cultivated in the arts. The gap in STEM education is teaching any process to apprehend, cultivate and develop kernels of inspiration, allowing technologists to see a vision of a different reality or to have a revelation that no one else sees or hears.

The church is a training ground for apprehending and processing inspiration. Unfortunately for technologists, the church has not effectively provided prophetic and inspiration examples in the technology marketplace, at least not since the 1700s. To make things worse, many church traditions embracing prophetic cultures shun education and are suspicious of technology. Most of us have seen prophetic art and dancing on stage during a worship service. But has anyone seen someone working out the details of a scientific breakthrough equation in the same church service? Aren't both revelations beautiful and powerful?

Underrepresenting technical revelation at church, coupled with the technologists' experience in a STEM education that undervalues mystery, discourages technically trained people from pursuing development of their revelatory gifts both at church and within their industry. Generally, technologists find churches do not often teach them how to express spiritual revelation in their workplaces because the language and culture of their church and the workplace are vastly different and mostly irrelevant to each other. Telling their boss God gave them a vision usually does not get the traction it deserves in the marketplace as it does in church. But that does not mean the message is less valuable in the marketplace; it means the message lacks the proper language and cultural context for the marketplace. Technologists need to be able to translate their prophetic inspirations and revelations from the church culture to their marketplace culture.

Let us dive deeper into this concept of the difference in language and culture between the church and technology marketplace. Within the Church, there is a common understanding and common language for spiritual and prophetic revelation. When we give a prophetic word to a Christian friend, we expect they will understand our heart is to provide them with a message that contains information for their good. They understand we are trying to communicate the Father's love to them. Further, we expect them to test the prophecy we give them to see if it is true and to apply what is true about what was said. When we get it wrong, the person kindly says it does not make sense to them. At the same time, even when we get it wrong, our pastors congratulate us for trying even though we did not successfully deliver a God-inspired message.

But telling your non-believing boss and co-workers that God gave you a solution is a different story. They do not have a framework or personal experience to understand the nature of prophecy and revelation. They do not know that we see in part and prophesy in part. When they hear "God said this or that," some turn away because the concept of a living God is unacceptable to them. Some have fantasy expectations about a divine revelation, like heaven breaking out in a Hallelujah chorus. Some might think when a technologist says God spoke something to them, that everything needs to be hundred percent true, and if there is any minor fault, the idea was not God's. Mostly, non-Christians in the technology marketplace are skeptical of God and especially that God speaks to people. Getting a revelation in the marketplace wrong only adds a reason for their skepticism. A Christian technologist in the marketplace, therefore, must frame the revelation within the worldview, culture, and language of their non-believing boss and co-workers.

Throughout this book, I use one of my experiences of advancing technology, from prophetic inspiration to seeing it implemented on the International Space Station. Using my experience, I hope to fill the inspiration gap in the education most technical people have about receiving inspiration, processing inspiration, bringing inspiration to their peers and workplace, and working through the development of inspiration to a viable concept, algorithm, or product. You will discover how technologists can use their prophetic gifting to advance technology within the marketplace and open a door for a meaningful discussion about God with their workmates and within their industry. Lastly, you will see how advancing technology escorts you before great men (reference Proverbs 18:16).

Introduction

I was fortunate to grow up in a small community of aerospace workers. There, the engineers, scientists, physicists, and technologists would gather at the hardware store for a cup of coffee and a discussion about what they worked on that week. The conversation might start by asking about fixing a plumbing, painting, or electrical problem at home. But within minutes, the conversation turned to the latest work on major government contracts. The hardware store was a daytime pub for people with pocket protectors. As a kid, I was exposed to seasoned scientists and engineers discussing in very specific detail about plumbing, painting, and electrical problems at home and a vast array of government-funded technology development. Listening to these discussions profoundly impacted me and instilled the idea that I could be a homeowner and aerospace technologist when I grew up.

While I grew up in the 1960s, I became aware of the Apollo program when I was nine years old. Suddenly, becoming an astronaut was my primary life ambition. Even today, I consider one of the greatest moments of my life was watching the Apollo 11 mission. Throughout that week and a half, I built a rocket from my Lego set, from my blocks, and my erector set. Becoming an astronaut was all I thought about. I learned astronauts needed a science Ph.D. and to be a fighter test pilot. Starting in fourth grade, I studied hard and learned all I could think about aeronautics. By fifth grade, I finished studying a college-level aerodynamics book that introduced me to calculus which I had to learn to understand to complete the homework at the end of the chapters.

I encountered several obstacles to performing well in school starting in second grade. My teacher noticed I would say different words when reading a book, and my reading comprehension was very low. She suggested I be tested for dyslexia. As it turns out, some dyslexic people jumble letters in only one or two directions. I jumble them up, down, back and forth, and diagonally, in all directions. Some people jumble only side by side; I jumble in a field of about one and a half inches. Some people jumble letters or numbers but not both. I jumble both. I was fortunate that I had a teacher that recognized dyslexia in the 1960s and that I was in a school system starting a program for dyslexia. For two years, I was in a special reading program. It included eye movement training, narrowing my field of attention when I read, and using my moving finger to keep my attention from wandering to different words and lines. Two times every day, I needed to practice these exercises for a minimum of forty-five minutes. After two years of special reading classes, I rejoined my classmates, but my reading skills, especially reading speed, even today, never really caught up to theirs.

Another learning problem was my attention. By fourth grade, teachers were telling my parents that I was easily distracted and had a hard time following multiple tasks and finishing assignments. Some might recognize this as Attention Deficit Disorder (ADD) or (ADHD) (H: Hyperactivity), but these were not common diagnoses in the 1960s. Instead, I was treated for a short time for only hyperactivity. While my behavior improved with medication, I felt lethargic and eventually bargained with my parents to get off the medicine in fourth grade if I behaved better in school.

While these setbacks often are insurmountable handicaps, they did not deter my dreams of being an astronaut, and somehow, I managed to perform well in school. My mom told me that given my challenges, if I still wanted to be an astronaut, I would have to double down and be smarter than anyone else. That is what I did, and for the most part, in grade school, I was the top student in most of my classes except reading and English. I felt I was still on my way to being an astronaut, having worked hard to compensate for dyslexia and ADHD.

Then, the summer before seventh grade, my world fell completely apart. I went to the doctor for my annual check-up, and they told me the worst news I could hear. He measured my height, manipulated a chart for a few seconds, and then told me an obstacle I was likely not going overcome or avoid; he told me how tall I would grow as an adult.

In those days, astronauts were selected from US Navy and US Air Force fighter and test pilot programs. The height limit for fighter and test pilots was five foot eight inches. Even though my family is tall, I never thought that would be an issue. The doctor told me I was going to be more than six feet tall. It crushed me. For a long time, in the back of my mind, I hoped he was wrong and that I still had a chance to be an astronaut. Halfway through seventh grade, the evidence was mounting that my height would disqualify me from being a fighter test pilot. I was devastated and completely gave up on my dream. If I couldn't become an astronaut, then I didn't need a Ph.D., so I gave up on school and stopped hanging out with the bright kids in school. Within a week, I went from the top scholastic performer to the worst.

I started high school just over the test pilot height limitation and in the remedial education programs because of my grades. Fortunately, I had a friend that helped me find a little more interest in school by appealing to my competitive nature. He bet me he could get better grades than I could in the classes we shared. I muddled through high school and most of a mechanical engineering degree, doing minimal work to get by. I was bored in school and found all but a few classes a learning disappointment. I wanted to be like the engineers and technologists in the hardware store, but I didn't feel like my education was leading me there. I thought school would teach me the things they knew. All I found in school was a repetition of things that did not mention a plumbing elbow, the benefits of oil base versus water-based paints, how to wire a three-way light switch, or developing a rocket motor for the space shuttle. Even my science classes let me down because all the experiments were not trying to find something new but rather reestablishing a known truth. The experiments in school were designed for a successful outcome. Still, I knew from the stories I heard and from my own experience at home that most experiments are unsuccessful or at least do not produce the expected outcome.

In my junior year at college, a major aircraft OEM offered an internship to me. My first responsibility was in an electrical engineering research group, where I demonstrated a knack for trying new ideas in our labs and developing prototypes. I was shortly put in charge of research, developing a specialized lab. I ended up leading a group and developed a lot of new technology in the following decade. I transferred to that company's space division and began working on the International Space Station (ISS). While I knew I would never go to the ISS myself, I found life satisfaction in enabling more than one hundred astronauts to live and work in orbit. Working in space programs and with astronauts might be the next best thing to being an astronaut. In many ways, I feel like I ended up where my ten-year-old self wanted to be.

Working on the ISS program, my career is best characterized by Psalms 75:6-7:

6 For exaltation comes neither from the east
Nor from the west nor from the south.
7 But God is the Judge:
He puts down one,
And exalts another.[4]

I am grateful to have God's favor resting on me. He has exalted me way beyond my capabilities and qualifications and beyond what my resume might suggest.

I joined the International Space Station (ISS) program as an expert in data and communication systems in severe and space environments. When I joined, I walked into a six-month-old problem that prevented the team from having a 99.7% confidence that the data and communication systems would work, which was required by the contract. There are many differences between the ISS data and communication systems

---

[4] The New King James Version. Nashville: Thomas Nelson. © 1982. (Ps 75:6,7).

and comparable terrestrial systems. The biggest difference is the ISS systems would not be completely assembled until the ISS was assembled in orbit. This meant the ISS data and communication system, unlike terrestrial systems that can be built, installed and tested in the building or premise, could not be tested and corrected as needed. Put more practically, when there is a problem with your fiber or cable at your house, your internet service provider (ISP) sends a technician for a local repair. The cost to the company might be $30 for fuel and the technician's time. In space, the fuel cost for one Shuttle launch to the ISS is about $60M.

Because the systems could not be tested before being assembled in space, the program needed an analysis tool that could guarantee the system's performance before even one part had been assembled. All common analysis tools considered showed that the largest systems would fail after on-orbit assembly, and the worst analysis result showed about one-third of the systems would fail before reaching the end of the ISS life. NASA programs are unique in that when a contractor has a problem meeting the contract requirements, NASA, the customer, sends help. When I started working on the ISS, NASA allocated over twenty-five people to solve the problem, and most had PhDs. I was intimidated, not so much by the problem, but by the education gap between my colleagues and myself.

If a solution could not be found, we would need to build a repeater that would condition and amplify the data signals. There has never been a repeater built for space. NASA and my company estimated it would have cost about twenty-five million dollars to design the repeater and redesign the data and communication systems. This would have potentially delayed the first launch of the ISS elements. There would be additional costs for the flight, logistics, and spare hardware, and the total impact was estimated to be about sixty million dollars. These data and communication systems not only carry all video, audio, and experimental data throughout the ISS but are integrated into the ISS navigation system. Simply put, without a working data and communication system, the ISS mission could be jeopardized.

I was on the program for about three months, and the team was turning its attention to the initial design of a repeater. Some of the team, including myself, was still working on developing an equation, but most felt it was a dead end. Unexpectantly, I had a dream that showed a mathematical function being processed over and over by a computer. The next morning, during my devotional time, I considered the dream. I ran into two problems trying to validate the technical merit of the dream. First, while I could write the mathematical function, it was math I had not been acquainted with. Second, while I took computer programming in school, the algorithm was not familiar because it functioned in a frequency domain rather than time. Therefore, I had to lean into my church experience and training in hearing God's voice and discerning if a message was from God. After my morning devotional, I knew my dream was a prophetic revelation, and I was convinced it was the solution to the problem even though I could not rationally explain it or communicate it to my team at work.

That morning I stepped into my boss's office and told him I knew I had the solution to the problem and told him about my dream. I also told him the solution used math and computer programming that I did not know. Nevertheless, I was convinced it was what we needed. He asked me how long it would take to figure out the details and how I knew it would work. I asked for six months and told him that I was convinced God gave me the dream. He said that since no one else had suggested any solution, mine, even though it seemed improbable, was the only option we had.

In the six months, I learned the equation in the dream was a probability distribution function and the repeating of the equation represented a Monte Carlo analysis. I was able to code a statistical analysis package into Microsoft Excel version 2 on the latest state-of-the-art (at the time) P80386 computer. I needed to make twenty-one system calculations that showed each data and communication system would work after it was assembled in orbit and for the fifteen-year design life.

Inspiration Insights

1. Yes, God cares about you, your career, and about the technology you are developing. It is just as easy for God to give revelation to advance technology at your work as it is to heal or encourage someone at your church.

2. Most of the time, you will not have the education, skills, or experience to evaluate your technical prophetic inspiration. However, you can rely on the skills and methods you learn at church to confirm the prophet revelations you receive. It's the same skill set but just a different application.

Science and Mystery

Too often, the church characterizes gaps between theology and perceptible life as a mystery. I had a conversation that started with a church leader friend saying, "[they] refuse to strive for what Jesus has freely given through the cross and His resurrection," pertaining to a health problem they were facing. As we in the church know, his statement is firmly based on a compilation of scriptures relating to divine health as well as other benefits gained by Jesus' death and resurrection. But the application overlays the life they perceived; they were sick and needed some medical attention.

Divine health is biblically true but not 100% true in our experience. Nevertheless, some Christians refuse to accept sickness as a 'truth' they have to live with. How does divine health theology play out when a mom who just gave birth to an unviable baby watches the baby, along with her dreams, fade away with each precious little breath? How does it fit in a community of terminally ill people or to people to whom God has revealed their final day? Perhaps a worse application would be someone who is ill and can be treated by typical medical intervention, but they decide the sickness is a lie and seeking medical intervention is 'striving.' I suspect, after hearing such proclamations of divine healing, any member of these groups could conclude that God does not care as much for them as He does for others. This is a huge theological contradiction unless you believe, as some traditions do that God's dispensation of grace is limited. These conclusions defame the God of all glory.

If your fallback when you are faced with gaps between theology and perceptible life is to explain it as 'mystery,' you embrace a theology that God is fickle about His promises instead of being expedient about them (reference 2 Peter 3:9). Maybe it is better to say we do not yet know rather than to classify it as a divine mystery. I am not saying there is no mystery, quite the opposite, as you will see! I want to distinguish between what is not explainable versus what God has hidden for us to find, what we cannot know versus what we should seek to know.

For me, mystery is an invitation to come and reason together with God; to taste and see the Lord is good (reference Isaiah 1:18, Psalms 34:8). Psalms 34:8 has an important limitation for searching for truth in mystery; that limitation is we must continuously respect the Lord. Proverbs 25:2 says God gives mystery for humanity to ponder until we understand. Bill Johnson, Leader of Bethel Church in Redding, California, frequently says, "God hides things for us, not from us."⁵ The Bible adds to this saying it is a glorious thing to explore the mysteries of our world and universe.

There is an interesting irony in the science and technology fields today. On the one hand, people advancing science agree with scripture that exploring mystery is noble and honorable. Marcel Gleiser, winner of the Templeton Prize, staff writer at Orbiter Magazine, and Dartmouth professor of natural philosophy, physics, and astronomy says, "…the very act of wondering about the behavior of the world, and how our minds can make sense of what we are able to see, is, as Einstein once remarked an act of veneration, inspired by what he called the 'cosmic religious feeling.'"⁶ Ironically, many scientists hope and believe their answers will inevitably show God doesn't exist. What they generally find is not less evidence that God exists but rather more and that there is more to understand.

One example of uncovering the truth in divine mystery is found in the rise of the nuclear age. Speaking of the end of days, 2 Peter 3:10 says, "…the elements will melt with fervent heat…" Up to the twentieth century, technologists and scientists considered this impossible. They could not imagine a heat that would dissociate an atom. Therefore, in the science versus Christian faith debate, the 'scientific fact' the elements

---

⁵ Johnson, Bill, "Dreaming with God: Co-Laboring with God for Cultural Transformation," Destiny Image Publishers, © 2006
⁶ Marcelo Gleiser, "Embracing the Mystery," Orbitermag.com, © 2019

could not melt was used to attack Biblical inerrancy. Specifically, since we 'know' the elements cannot melt, 2 Peter 3:10 says they do, the Bible must be wrong, and the Bible fallible. However, during the rise of the atomic age, scientists learned both fission and fusion have enough released heat to dissociate and reform elements. This is fundamental in using the energy from these atomic processes. This discovery thus substantiated the biblical claim, "The elements will melt," and that science, before the nuclear age, was wrong. Since science is propositional, science will adapt and change when the next proposition better describes, represents, and demonstrates the reality we know.

Propositions are the start of the scientific method. As children, we are taught a basic construct of the scientific method that might be represented, as shown in Figure 1. As education continues, technologists and scientists are taught how to make and refine a hypothesis, test methods and standards for creating experiments to validate a hypothesis, including limiting experimental variables, experimental discipline, data reduction techniques, how to qualify data, and finally, how to write a technical report for a peer review. We are taught this version of the scientific method because it aligns with the tools and skills schools can teach.

I want to bring attention to what this version of the scientific process does not show; it does not show how the experimenter or investigator was inspired to start the investigation or if they were inspired before or during the process.

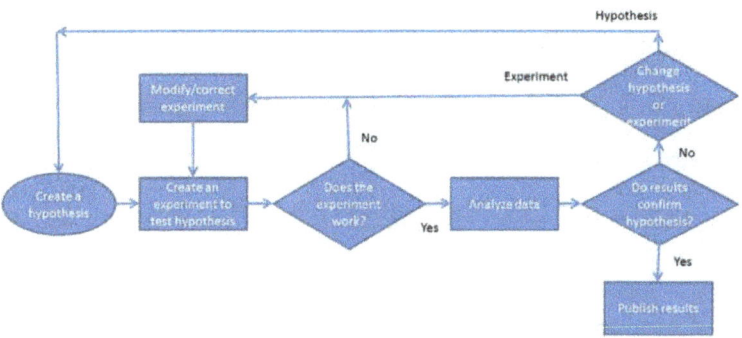

Figure 1: Scientific Method Flowchart

Cartoons show Sir Isaac Newton sitting under a fruit tree when he is hit in the head with a piece of falling fruit. Suddenly he understood gravity and the laws of motion. I am here to tell you scientific inspiration and advancement do not happen that way.

The missing and critical step, or steps not shown in Figure 1, is how the investigator is inspired by an idea that goes beyond the things they learned or experienced. If the investigator stays within the realm of what they know, they will never advance science and technology. Somehow, the investigator must embrace an idea rooted in the unknown; they must delve into the depth of mystery that has no current scientific foundation or logic.

Therefore, the hypothesis of scientific advancement is not a projection of known science; it is an inquiry into mystery. After a hypothesis is formed, the scientific method provides a methodology and framework for establishing and proving the inspiration from mystery.

Inspiration is not limited to the processes that form an original hypothesis; inspiration is common for both unknown evolutionary and sometimes revolutionary methods of solving problems. The history of the evolution of science can easily be framed in the view that God wants to tell humanity His secrets. And who is best prepared to receive God's secrets than God's people who practice prayer and meditation and are maturing active gifts of revelation?

Some may argue against spiritual revelation, especially spiritual gifts of revelation (prophecy, knowledge, and wisdom). They might draw from 1 Corinthians 14, saying the passage clearly shows that gifts are only used in a church context. However, Paul is clearly writing to a church he desperately wants to be the best example of Christ because, literally, the entire world passed through Corinth. Nowhere in

1 Corinthians 12-14 or Romans 12 do we find Paul saying spiritual gifts are exclusively limited to the church. These discussions are rooted in the church as the backdrop and the intended audience. In the same way, I am writing to Christian technologists and have not addressed modern artists, so Paul wrote to the church and not to other social, government, and industrial groups. That is not to say the concepts are irrelevant to other situations and applications.

So, the only instruction we have from the New Testament is in a church-specific context without any specific secular or religious delineation. Moses, when building the tabernacle, drew skilled craftspeople from the marketplace. Exodus 35:30 tells us Moses enlisted Bezalel, the son of Uri because God had 'filled them with the Spirit of God, in wisdom and understanding, in knowledge and all manner of workmanship (wood, metal, and precious stones.') Note that God told Moses to draw from the secular and not from the religious community. Today, we are preparing people to hear from God in church and sending them into the marketplace to advance humanity through divine inspiration integrated with science and technology as a testimony of God and His Kingdom.

Getting back to the scientific method, we have established technologists can receive prophetic inspiration at any time during the scientific or development process. We focused on the initial revelation that begins the scientific investigation. In my ISS example, a revelation came in the middle of the development of a major NASA program. In that case, a revelation was needed before it was accepted in the respective communities. Further, the proof of the revelation relied on the disciplines within the scientific method because that is the common culture and language of technology.

Revelation and inspiration are not always directed through dreams, visions, and other communications to your spirit or mind. Sometimes they are revealed in your subconscious and in the quiet places of your being. Often you are surprised when those revelations and inspirations bubble up to your consciousness or awareness.

The ISS data communication cable was made of expensive and somewhat exotic materials that would survive the space environments and use conditions. These materials were not typically used for the terrestrial equivalents. These materials like to shrink, which can cause signal degradation and shorten the life of the data link. The team thought preshrinking the bulk cable before building the harnesses would limit the shrinkage after the harnesses were built. However, the process of shrinking the bulk cable was laborious and took several days of eight hours shifts.

One day at my desk, I noticed a loose thread on my shirt and meant to pull it out but ended up pulling a little more than a foot before deciding to cut it. While I was proofreading a report on a completely different topic, I started fidgeting with the thread. Before long, I unconsciously drew the thread weaving it through my fingers. A coworker and friend passing my desk asked me what I was doing. When I looked up over my thread-woven hand to answer, I saw in my mind's eye the way we could condition the communication cable more efficiently.

The thread in my hand inspired a pulley design that allowed the cable to be continuously drawn into a cold chamber and then drawn to a hot chamber multiple times. This was much more effective than manually conditioning the cable and was performed in less than half the time because it could run twenty-four hours a day.

I am not sure if the thread inspiration was prophetic, a daydream, or just my fidgeting. However, I want to emphasize the importance of paying attention to the unconscious things you do and allowing yourself to be surprised. I suspect many advances are stumbled upon indirectly rather than through dedicated brainstorming sessions. Just like when we heighten our sense of spiritual alertness when we are in a prophetic conference at church, we can similarly pay attention to what is happening in the spiritual world at our workplace, in our garages, or while paddling to the next wave.

Inspiration Insights

1. God invites technologists to explore the mystery. God is not shy about explaining His creation, and He delights in talking about and revealing it.

2. The scientific method is a discipline of developing a kernel of inspiration into a body of data, conclusions, and typically a report that can be peer-reviewed or published. It does not give any insight into the process of technical inspiration that forms the hypothesis.

3. Prophetic inspiration is not limited to the beginning of the scientific process; it can come at any time and is useful at any point in scientific discovery and advancement.

4. Prophetic inspiration in church or the marketplace can come from a dream, a song, a conversation, or even from fidgeting. It is important to allow your spirit to be curious and continuously prompt your spirit to be aware in all the things you do… especially take note of your unconscious from time to time.

Inspiration

"...we are rapidly moving into the age of creation intensification."

Tom Peters[7]

What do Guglielmo Marconi, Gene Rodenberry, Jack Kilby, and Steve Jobs have in common? They contributed to today's personal infotainment devices, sometimes called mobile phones. Mobile phone technology fundamentally and significantly changed the way we live. But we are not talking about mobile devices; we are talking about inspiration. Each of these technologists was inspired to think beyond the technology of their day. This way of thinking is what the US Patents' office used to call a 'Flash of Genius.' The Flash of Genius doctrine gave legal patent guidelines based on an inventive act coming to the mind of the inventor. Today, the criteria are based on the idea of being 'non-obvious.'

Marconi imagined, developed, and patented a method for RF transmission and reception of information. Gene Rodenberry imaged a portable personal communication device that could be carried by the user. Jack Kilby imagined,

---

[7] Tom Peters, "Reimage Business Excellence in a Disruptive Age", Better Life Media, © 2004

developed, and patented a method of building microcircuits. And Steve Jobs imagined, developed, and patented the iPhone[8]. Inspiration was a key ability to see a problem differently from their contemporaries.

Robert Kearns, the inventor of intermittent windshield wipers, was driving home one rainy night. He found his car's windshield wipers, even in the low setting, were too vigorous for the rain that was falling that night. The streaks from the raindrops on the windshield made it difficult for him to see the road. He went home, and for the next several months, he designed the intermittent windshield wiper controller that was modeled after the blinking action of the human eye. He developed the intermittent control circuit in his garage because his job responsibilities at the Ford Motor Company did not afford the opportunity and time needed to develop his technology. His solution was a vision of the windshield wipers that worked periodically rather than continuously.

Many people enter STEM education to change the world and possibly have a career aligned with their passions. Sadly, few find those jobs after they graduate. As technologists develop their careers, they find many companies do not have salary-competitive career paths in technology as they have for management. Consequently, like Robert Kerns, many STEM

---

[8] US Patent D228,756 S

students tend to grow out of technology careers as their careers advance. They enter line management, program management, quality assurance, and other non-technical positions in their companies. To be sure, these positions are important, but they may not give a technologist frequent opportunities to develop breakthrough technology. All too often, technologists find themselves in positions requiring little or no technical inspiration.

Working in roles and responsibilities that do not tap into the imagination of the technologist is a least one factor that decreases patent productivity as technologists age, as shown in Figure 2. If innovation was dependent on education and experience, you would expect patent rates to increase as seniority increases. You would expect people with more technology experience would be more creative and capable of getting new patents. However, it appears the more experienced the technologist, the less inspired they become.

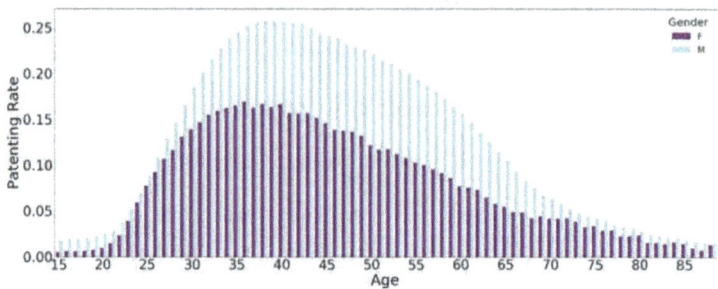

Figure 2 - Patent productivity with respect to age[9]

Lower patent productivity with respect to age is contrary to Joel 2:28, which says, "I will pour out my Spirit on all people. Your sons and daughters will prophesy, your old men will dream dreams, your young men will see visions." It is clear Joel expected innovation to come from the Spirit of God, not education or experience. I am not suggesting the decline in patent productivity means older technologists are losing their spirituality. However, while Joel predicts steady rates of inspiration between young and old people, somehow, older technologists are not as effective in getting and transitioning inspiration and innovation into the marketplace.

---

[9] The Age of Invention: Matching Inventor Ages to Paten Based on Web Scraped Sources, pg 11, National Bureau of Economic Research, Cambridge, MA, © 2021,
https://www.nber.org/system/files/working_papers/w28768/w28768.pdf

So let us begin a discussion on how to receive inspiration. My career success is largely due to the prophetic inspiration that I successfully brought to my workplace. How did this start? My grade school teachers used to say I daydreamed too much, and I would get negative remarks on my report card. By high school, after years of being scolded for daydreaming, being distracted, and being inattentive, the negative comments stopped. While this made me a better student in the evaluation of the educational system, it decreased the frequency of inspiration that was reflected in my hobbies.

I can tell you that most of my 'daydreaming' was thinking and imagining solutions for the things I was designing and building at home. I suspect if only one teacher had asked me what I was daydreaming about, they might have seen it as an educational opportunity rather than a distraction from their curriculum. With the sad priority of education being memorizing facts and figures, creativity gets pushed behind. In grade school, I had many airplane, chemistry, electrical, and mechanical projects ranging from building my own fireworks to designing and building my own free-flight airplanes. When I graduated from high school, my hobbies reduced to car restoration requiring very little inspiration.

Our educational system does not teach creativity. A NASA study found that of 1,600 four and five-year-olds, ninety-eight percent scored at a 'creative genius' level. Five years later, only thirty percent of the same group of children scored at the same level, and again, after another five years, only twelve percent. When the same test was administered to adults, it was found that only two percent scored at this genius level.[10] It says in the Inc. magazine article, "To Regain Creativity," Land and Beth suggested "let your mind wander..." and explained the reason kids are creative is that they are daydreamers.

Could it be 'daydreaming' is really the first step in learning how to receive prophetic inspiration? For me, I knew the answers I needed for my projects at home were beyond my education and beyond the information readily available through the encyclopedia. I was training myself to receive prophetic inspiration though I did not have a framework to understand it that way, nor any Christian theology of spiritual gifts for that matter.

By high school and college, I hated being called a daydreamer. I determined daydreaming was not valuable and adopted the common notion that discovery and invention were gained through the ninety-nine percent part of genius, perspiration that Thomas Edison talked about. After falling in love with Jesus in college, I was introduced to the gifts of

---

[10] Land, George & Beth, Jerimiah, "Breakpoint and Beyond: Mastering the Future Today", Harper Collins Publishers, © 1992

prophecy and words of knowledge. After some time, I started leading worship, revelation, and prayer meetings. I was not very good at unpacking spiritual downloads on the spot, so I developed a habit of preparation. Mowing my lawn was my method of choice. Mowing the lawn was not some Zen mystical experience. It is a mindless activity that requires a certain amount of time and allows me to begin to 'daydream' again.

I began by focusing on specific people and circumstances and prayerfully asking God if there was a message I could bring that could help or encourage them. Often the messages I received encouraged and built up the group I was ministering to. 'Daydreaming' while mowing the lawn was the beginning of a regular prophetic rhythm. It seeded a desire for giving prophetic revelation in a broader scope than what was typical in my small groups. In those days, I would never have imagined bringing the gifts of wisdom, knowledge, and prophecy to the marketplace.

Some might argue by focusing on the people I knew and their situation. My lawn-mowing daydreaming was not prophetic inspiration at all. Maybe so. Nevertheless, it is important you define spiritual gifts so they are attainable through faith. It is improper theology to define spiritual gifts in ways that make them impossible or improbable for the believer.

My engineering school did not have enough dorm space, and I was happy to stay in the dorms of a nearby Christian college. That college had a very conservative dispensational theology, which included the cessation of miracles and spiritual gifts when the apostles died. Specifically, they taught miracles were only done by Jesus and the apostles and added they are always one hundred percent complete and achieved instantaneously. I, coming from a neo-charismatic tradition believing all the spiritual gifts are demonstrated and available today, did not agree with their definition. Their definition is not biblical. First, Elisha, not Jesus or the apostles, did not bother going to Naaman but instead gave instructions to dip seven times in the Jordon (2 Kings 5). This miracle took place well after Elisha issued the instructions. Therefore, the miracle was not instantaneous. The blind man in Mark 16 experienced incremental steps to regain his sight. This contradicts both the instantaneous and hundred percent requirements the college taught. The ten lepers in Luke 17 were healed after Jesus said to show themselves to the priests, "…as they went, they were cleansed." Once again, the miracle was not instantaneous. I cannot say why this particular school taught that theology, but I am certain of this; their definition of miracles prevented their students from praying for miracles. In his book, '*Surprised by the*

Holy Spirit,' John White (a talented author unlike myself) writes people do not see miracles because they do not have a worldview that allows for miracles. For me, the birth of my two kids was a miracle. For the medical staff, it was another day at work. Which perspective helped make them the special people they are today?

If you define prophecy in a way that will be next to impossible for you to be prophetic, you will likely not be prophetic because of your own definition, not because you are incapable of receiving a prophetic message. Like the example of the cessationist theology of miracles, your definition excludes the Romans and 1 Corinthians passages, with whom Paul writes instructions about the proper administration of prophecy, words of wisdom, and words of knowledge in the church. Note in those texts, the Roman and especially the 1 Corinthian audience were already ministering to each other in those spiritual gifts.

In the end, your definition of prophecy is much less important than the outcome of your practice. The outcome of my lawn-mowing daydreams helped hundreds of people. While I often started my daydreams with people I knew, by the last strip of lawn to mow, I often received messages from people I knew nothing about. They saw the power of God demonstrated because they received a critically personal message, sometimes on their first visits to our meetings.

In a workplace productivity article, Kerry Law says, "…forty percent of creative ideas occurred when participants were engaged in activities that allowed their minds to wander."[11] But daydreaming is only the tip of the creative iceberg.

I had the wonderful opportunity to go to Vanguard University for a Ministry, Religion, and Leadership degree. This gave me an opportunity to research what I called the seed of prophetic utterance. My initial hypothesis was the kernel of prophetic revelation was similar to most people who would have a similar inspiration experience. I interviewed about twenty prophetic people and found the kernel of prophetic inspiration is oriented to each individual and changes all the time for most prophetic people. I commonly heard, "I get a few words, and I prayerfully press into those words," and "I see pictures that I know are for a specific person or situation." Some described a physical sensation (warmth, tingling, heightened heartbeats with a highlight on a person or group) that validated a notion that popped into their heads. Dreams were not as common as you might think. However, I heard

---

[11] Law, Kerry, "Why staring out the window is the work habit you need - not a waste of time", Metro.co.uk, metro-lifestyle, © 2022.

prophets seeing visions overlaying reality in a way that highlighted the difference between the kingdoms of God and of Earth. Prophetic worship leaders sometimes mentioned feeling one phrase of a song had a special significance, and they would repeat the line while pressing into the significance. One thing I found surprising was many long-time prophetic people like Dick Mills, while having a known and characteristic form of delivery, said God communicates the kernel in different ways. I suppose this is because if the kernel was the same, the prophetic gift would become routine and not require faith. I concluded the initial seed of prophetic inspiration is more associated with the prophet than a uniform process that renders multitudes of prophetic seeds.

The same is true for prophetic inspiration in the marketplace. I wrote of my daydreaming as a child, but God faithfully challenges me with new places and methods of inspiration. Talking to a fellow Christian technologist about his inspiration, he first received inspiration during his prayer and quiet time. Like me, he says the method of his inspiration evolved over the years. Another friend says he worked on a project for a couple of years. Over that time, it changed direction from the original goal as a result of many incremental inspirations but turned out to generate several patents. He likens the project to the adhesive used on 3M's Post-It notes, which was supposed to be permanent ski-binding adhesive.

The application came from Art Fry, a friend of Dr. Spencer Silver, who invented what they both considered useless non-permanent adhesive. Mr. Fry, part of a church choir, inserted small paper notes in his hymnals during Wednesday's practice, but they would fall out by Sunday. Together, Mr. Fry and Mr. Silver made small paper pieces with their non-permanent adhesive and distributed them to the church choir and all over 3M, where they worked. These examples emphasize inspiration is not always instantaneous. My friend explained his long-term product development as a series of 'micro-revelations' that led to a technology shift over a couple of years.

I was diagnosed with an aggressive form of prostate cancer in 2018. My doctor suggested picking one of four treatment plans. I was aware of two others that the doctor was willing to support through a referral. I needed to decide quickly because the affected area was relatively large, and the cancer was aggressive. Throughout that day, I notified my kids and closest friends, asking for prayer. I set that evening aside to research and select a treatment.

That same day I received a CD, 'Revealing Jesus' by Hillsong. I turned it on as I started my treatment plan research. It looped for a second time, and while I was reading and studying about cancer treatment, the Holy Spirit called my attention to the first song, 'In Jesus' Name.' I can't explain why

I didn't hear the song the first or second time. In the song, Darlene Zschech breaks into a prophetic word and makes several declarations near the end of the song about cancer being healed. At that moment, I was convinced God would heal me no matter what treatment I picked.

I know Darlene Zschech didn't have me in mind. I know she was speaking to people in the audience the night of the recording. I know we are effectively worlds apart, and she could not practically know my condition. I know her declarations were made five years before I heard the song. I know these are some of the reasons a skeptic would suggest it was all a giant coincidence. But I know the Shepherd's voice, and He spoke to me about being healed.

Right after the revelation, my concerned son called. I had the choice to tell him I was not sure of the outcome, which was the scientific and medical reality, or tell him I was going to be okay because God revealed He would heal me. I told him God was not going to allow this to be the end of me and that it was only a speed bump. I don't know how Darlene Zschech received her word or why they included it in the recording. What I know is that the Holy Spirit started a process by calling my attention to the song that resulted in a prophetic declaration over my life. Prophetic inspiration comes in many forms, and I suspect we only catch a small portion. Being an active listener to the Holy Spirit is the key to getting spiritual revelation.

Before I give some advice about learning how God communicates prophetic revelation, I want to dispel the idea that prophetic revelation and inspiration are limited. For that to be true:

1. God would have to be somehow limited, and He is not.

2. God would have to be disinterested in humanity's needs or disinterested in our interests, and He is not.

3. That God only communicates to certain people, but he doesn't; He wants to be in a relationship with all people.

Therefore, prophetic inspiration is available to everyone, even technologists.

With that in mind, I suggest hanging around prophetic people at church. Recognize their ministry to the church is different from your ministry to the marketplace. These have two different languages and cultures. Therefore, the language of the marketplace will be different from the language of the church.

Church culture lays an infrastructure for hearing, understanding, evaluating, processing, and acting on the prophetic utterance. The marketplace has a different culture which does not include a Christian understanding of prophetic utterances. Therefore, a Christian technologist needs to unpack prophetic inspiration differently in the marketplace.

1 Sam 19:18-24 talks about the 'school of the prophets' where young prophets would live and fellowship with seasoned prophets. There is so much to say about the importance of fellowship while developing spiritual gifts, but I will summarize by repeating what I learned from John Wimber; 'spiritual things are easier caught than taught.' In time, you WILL 'catch' it when you spend time with similarly gifted people.

Secondly, vary the way you spend time with God. 1 Kings 19 tells us that after defeating the prophets of Baal, Elijah fled to a small tree, had an encounter with a heavenly host, and then went to the mountain. There he hid in a cave wanting to hear God. He expected God's voice in the wind, earthquake, and fire. But God did not speak in those events. Finally, Elijah is surprised to hear God speak in a 'still small voice.' Notice that Elijah expected something loud and overwhelming. My assumption is Elijah, up to this time in his prophetic career, always heard God's voice clearly distinguishable from anything other than 'sound.' It was different this time. Force yourself to find new places, processes, and practices for inspiration because, from what I have learned, God communicates in ways that will stretch your faith.

Inspiration Insights

1. Define spiritual gifts, especially revelation gifts (knowledge, wisdom, and prophecy), to align with scripture and in a way that makes them accessible to you.

2. The kernel of prophetic inspiration will always challenge your faith. Even seasoned prophets rely on faith, not their revelation experience. Expect the unexpected.

3. The tools and methods you use to determine prophetic inspiration from God in the church are the same tools you use to determine if marketplace prophetic inspiration is from God.

4. Hang around prophetically gifted people to develop your own gift.

Testing and Proving

"Beloved, do not believe every spirit, but test the spirits, whether they are of God because many false prophets have gone out into the world."[12]

The marketplace has barriers to prophetic inspiration the church does not. This chapter lists a few: your reputation, our coworker's skepticism of God and His revelations, if the prophetic inspiration is relevant, and the morality of the prophetic inspiration's application. Intermixed are tips for gaining confidence in your prophetic inspiration. We also consider how the brain works in a relationship is added because many immerging marketplace prophetic people are sensitive about knowing if God really spoke to them.

Reputation

Nothing will undermine your opportunity to communicate divine revelation more than a bad reputation. This is true in the church and the marketplace. The difference is the church is supposed to forgive, but the marketplace has no expectation of forgiveness, and secular people rarely forget a Christian's hypocrisy. In fact, they are quick to point it out.

---

[12] The New King James Version. Nashville: Thomas Nelson. © 1982. (1 Jn 4:1).

Since communicating prophetic inspiration starts with our bosses, peers, and workmates, we need to:

1. Have good character at work and respectfully live out our Christian values and morals.

2. Bring love and life to our workmates and places of business.

3. Create an environment allowing dialog and discourse on out-of-the-box ideas, no matter the source.

4. Be prepared for and open to criticism of your revelation.

5. Build your boss's and workmate's confidence in your work, work habits, and commitment to your organization.

6. Be supportive of people and your employer.

7. Exercise wisdom.

8. Maintain these commitments on your social media platforms.

We have a responsibility and obligation to bolster God's name and reputation as His representatives and ambassadors.

We have established we can receive divine prophetic inspiration to help our companies succeed, which in turn, usually helps us succeed. The next step after receiving a prophetic inspiration is to verify if it is from God. Technologists and scientists will want to lean into their rational tools and skills to evaluate a prophetic revelation. However, there is no 'Spirit of God-ometer' where the input is our revelation, and the output is "True" or "False." This evaluation comes from your spiritual discernment, discernment that has been developed at your church.

1 John 4:1 tells us to test the 'spirits' to see if they are from God. The Ephesian church is commended for testing the apostles (Revelations 2:2). In the church, it is easy to get feedback regarding a vision, prophetic work, or word of knowledge. You will be fortunate to have a Christian coworker whom you can consult with to evaluate your revelation. However, most of the time, you will find you will be the final, if not the only, decision-maker regarding the source of your revelation. While both the church and the marketplace will test your prophetic inspiration, the evaluation criteria are vastly different.

In the church, some common evaluation criteria are, does the word edify and build up, is it useful for the recipient, is it relevant to the recipient, and is it communicated in a way that can be implemented? Commonly, prophetic people will ask if what they said means something to the person to whom they minister. Our gracious and loving church family has a common culture that understands we sometimes need affirmation when we try to communicate a divine message. Sometimes we get it wrong, and our church family will forgive and forget, especially when we are learning to communicate our inspiration.

The marketplace evaluates your prophetic inspiration on its effectiveness and relevance to the business. This evaluation is long after you discern if your revelation is from God. As it is in the church, this first step is mostly the 'prophet' assessing the kernel of inspiration to decide to move forward, get more revelation to supplement gaps or underdeveloped revelation, or wait until you understand the revelation's purpose better. Your church experience will guide you in determining if the revelation has a divine origin.

The next step is to translate the revelation into the marketplace jargon. Usually, your revelation is mostly non-verbal, or the significant content is not language based. Therefore, to communicate your revelation to those who will evaluate its relevance, business value, and usefulness, you need to mature the kernel of inspiration by translating it into the language your boss and peers understand and are fluent. From that point, you become a champion of the revelation. This is generally a very high-level explanation of what your revelation is in your marketplace language. It might include contrasts to similar solutions or ideas and how your revelation is superior to those former methods, or it might be an extension of a previous method, solution, idea, or process. If you can, you should include a value proposition. In industrial science and technology, value can be patents, competitive advantage, cost reduction, or breaking a barrier technical or scientific barrier. Developing your revelation or inspiration is important because your bosses and peers probably do not have the revelation skills and communication skills you have.

No matter how prepared you are when you talk to your bosses and peers, they will have questions. They will ask if your revelation advances your companies program or directives, it will give a competitive advantage, and how it can be monetized. Your peers will consider if this is the right time to pursue this revelation if there are there any enabling resources or technologies needed to be successful. Our workmates' culture is relentlessly pragmatic, performance, and results-driven. Therefore, we have a responsibility to verify what we claim is divinely inspired and mitigate risk.

Technology Marketplace Skepticism

The marketplace is intolerant of us getting it wrong. This creates an adverse and austere environment for prophetic revelation. Matthew 13:57 shows us unbelief is a powerful deterrent to supernatural ministry. To worsen the climate for prophetic inspiration, our unsaved fellow technologists and scientists are specifically critical of God and His people. This unbelief and hostility toward the miraculous creates environments that even limit Jesus' ministry. Furthermore, even when we get divine revelation right, most of our workmates remain skeptical, if not critical, that God was the initiator. They would rather ascribe the revelation to hard work, some natural phenomenon, or even other gods. But these, our technology community, are the same people that need to know Jesus and whom the Father wants us to reveal His love, glory, majesty, and miracles.

Because the marketplace culture is more critical of prophetic inspiration, it is important for us to get clarity on the prophetic kernel of inspiration. To be sure, the more experience you have with prophetic revelation either at church or the marketplace, the more tools you have to validate your revelation from God. This does not mean gaining prophetic inspiration and telling the marketplace is ever easy. You always share the revelation with a measure of faith.

Relevance

When you receive marketplace revelation, make sure it is relevant to your work situation. The task at hand is to evaluate something. This is often non-verbal, embedded in a framework of your spirituality, and will have some elements rooted in the culture of your spiritual experience and language. Seasoned prophets easily distinguish prophetic downloads from their imaginations. Confirming the prophetic kernel, like the nature of the kernel itself, is as unique as you are, but there seem to be some common evaluation themes worth mentioning.

Prophetic people often tell of physical manifestations that confirm their kernels of inspiration. Some examples are feeling a stirring in the gut or chest, feeling warmth or coolness that comes and goes, and feeling something in the face or sinuses akin to a sneeze without the irritation. Some, especially those in healing ministry, report having sympathetic symptoms that come suddenly. Some say they get a sort of tunnel vision that focuses on the prophetic subject. Others report experiencing tingling in all or a part of their bodies.

Other prophetic people say they have a mental or emotional process to confirm prophetic kernels. They might get divine confidence, they see how the kernel fits like a puzzle piece into the bigger story, some get moments of acute clarity while others report an obscuration of everything unrelated to the subject problem associated with the prophetic inspiration. Others say they just "know in their knower." Dick Mills reported he often saw the kernel of inspiration associated with specific scripture revealing the kernel's application and truth.

Sometimes, but rarely in my experience, God might simply confirm by direct and sometimes "audible" communication. Direct communications seem to be associated with urgency or warning. Other times, technologists are in the right place at the right time, sometimes to save people's lives.

I was on a full airplane and smelled a unique scent from a problem I had investigated many years earlier. I knew what was happening right away and what the next steps should be. I called the flight attendant to let her know how to avoid a fire inside the cabin.

The FAA conducted fire safety investigations and found that aircraft cabins become toxic two minutes after a fire starts. From a cruising altitude of roughly 35000 feet, a jetliner takes about two minutes to fall out of the sky. That means a cabin fire in flight will likely kill everyone on board if not for the onboard safety equipment. As with every revelation in the marketplace, the flight attendant asked how I knew about the danger. I explained I used to work for the builder of the aircraft and was a principal investigator for this problem. At the time, I was a designated engineering representative to the FAA.

Notice, that my 'revelation' to the flight attendant was validated by my credentials. This is true of experts like myself in that flight situation as much as it is true with your prophetic revelations. Your prophetic revelations will be validated by your credentials. The credentials for your prophetic revelation in the marketplace are your reputation. how effectively you communicate the merits of the revelation within the context of your workplace language and culture and your previous successes.

While this was a dramatic example of an urgent situation, most technologists work where change happens slowly. This allows technologists time to process and develop the kernel of revelation.

Confidence in hearing God's voice

At this point, it is worth discussing some common processes of receiving and processing a kernel of revelation. Let's start by talking about how hearing God's voice becomes easier.

Our physical brains are predisposed to make relationship connections. From the day we are born, our brain rewires itself through relationship experiences to be more relational; the more time in a relationship with a person, the more physically "wired" our brains become to that person. Sadly, many people live isolated lives where these connections are not formed in their brains. As a result, their brains never learn to connect with people.

These neurological pathways forming relational bonds are produced by neuropeptides; chemical messengers that are made up of amino acid chains that are released by the neurons in the brain; Oxytocin, predominantly in females, and

Vasopressin, predominantly in males, promote bonding[13] and emotional attachment. In effect, our minds will become hardwired to those we grow close to. This might be why you can get a call from an old friend you haven't heard from for a long time and pick up right where you left off.

SPECT brain scans show, in real-time, the active and inactive portions of the brain. They have been used to dramatically show brain damage and how the brain is affected by different drugs and alcohol. Neurotheology researchers in the US and Canada used SPECT scans of many people's brains and found that "the brains of people who spend untold hours in prayer and meditation are different[14]", and the active areas of their brains mimic those with whom they have long-term relationships and their loved ones. They concluded your brain is being rewired by the relationship you have with God, especially in prayer and meditation. Therefore, you are more likely to discern God's voice the longer you are in a relationship with Him!

The tools and techniques we are discussing throughout this book are common and can be useful, especially when you are starting your prophetic journey. However, they are only

---

[13] Young, Wang, Zuoxin, "The neurobiology of pair bonding". Nature Neuroscience. 7 (10): 1048–1054 © 2004.
[14] B. Hagerty, "Prayer May Reshape Your Brain and Your Reality", NPR special series, The Science of Spirituality, © 2009.

primers and temporarily useful while you develop your own patterns for receiving and testing revelation. While God created us to be in a relationship with Him, ultimately, God wants His prophets, whether to the church or the marketplace, to fundamentally act on His voice while growing in faith. In short, God wants us to proclaim divine revelation with lesser reliance on the tools, techniques, or systems and greater reliance and confidence in His voice. That confidence only comes with practice and experience of repeated prayer and communion with our heavenly Father.

Consider the Romans 12 passage on spiritual gifts; note prophecy is the only gift that is exercised in accordance with the measure of the person's faith. When Paul lists the other gifts, they are in accordance with their execution target. For example, the next gift Paul mentions in the Romans list is the gift of ministry. Paul says to use the gift of ministry in your ministering. If the exercise of spiritual gifts was rooted in experience, a system, tools, or techniques, Romans 12 would have said so. I suspect Paul specifically indicates the execution of prophecy is by faith to differentiate it from a skill or technique. It is critical to understand your faith is developed by your journey and that your journey is different from mine. The one thing that is common is the Holy Spirit is directing both of our journeys to develop a deeper faith in each of us. In my research on the kernel of prophecy, the Holy Spirit forever changes the methods and natures of the kernels of revelation. It was reported to me that these changes caused the prophets' faith to grow. Today's mustard seed of faith is not tomorrow's.

Morality

Many technologists and scientists should consider the morality of prophetic inspiration within the context of its application. Generally, analyzing the morality of prophetic revelation in the church is simply asking if the message is encouraging and/or strengthening a person or group. The optics are much different in the marketplace. We must consider the end product's application and intended use.

To be sure, most of the raw technology developed for the programs at work is amoral. Similarly, divinely revealed technology is equally amoral. Issues of morality come in the application of technology and become more critical when we work in the defense industry. Therefore, the application of your prophetic revelation should be considered. The questions I ask are:

- Can the application of this revelation and technology kill innocent people?

- Can the product being developed be copied or stolen and used in an immoral application?

- Will my company or government control the developed product in moral and humane ways?
- What will happen if the revelation and associated technology are misused in immoral ways?
- Will the technology be managed so its application is for humanity's good?

Early in my career, I worked for defense contractors and started developing some technology that caught the interest of the US Department of Defense. At first, I rationalized developing weapons technology with two arguments:

- If God revealed something that advanced technology, He must approve its application in my context. I deferred the moral responsibility to the fact I was receiving revelation that supported the project.
- It was my patriotic duty to develop the highest level of technology possible for the defense projects rationalizing that I was not morally responsible for how the technologies might be used.

Notice I did not take any responsibility for the morality of the application of the revelations I received while developing the technology for the defense projects.

After a few years, I learned my government had given some of the products containing the technology I developed to a country I knew had little moral constraints. I struggled with the moral implications. I realized my deferral of moral responsibility was directly responsible for the technological advancements and its potential for an immoral end-use. That dilemma forced me to ask if I should continue in the defense industry.

There is a lot packed into career decisions, and my choices will be different than yours. At that time, I decided to change career paths. This decision came with a salary cut which was hard to accept when my family was young and I was the primary wage earner. It also meant that I had to take a demotion. It took about five years to get back to an equivalent seniority, position, and salary. My spouse and I never regretted discussing the morality of my career choice.

Morality in defense contracting has become an important issue. Some defense contractors today, while interviewing a candidate, will ask if they have any moral objections to the work and its application. Every technologist should think about the morality of their products, especially Christians.

The defense industry is not the only industry with morality concerns. A songwriter friend's band had a record label contract. His cross-over band focused on indirect evangelism to reach the lost. Their music and lyrics were not overtly church-focused and avoided Christianese words. The lyrics had Christian values and themes overlaying the story and theme of the song in hopes of inspiring people to look for answers beyond themselves and to look to God.

The recording label was fully secular. My friend was concerned that by signing the rights to the songs to the secular recording label, his songs might be marketed to immoral places like strip clubs, pornographic movies, or worse. He resolved the dilemma by continuing to write the songs and trusting God to direct the music to the people that needed it, even in the strip clubs or pornographic movies.

Everyone's optics for the moral implications of their revelations will be different. I shared mine as an example that morality is important to consider and that the choice may have real consequences for you and your family. While I moved away from defense to space, you might come to a completely different decision. To be sure, what shapes your decision will be and should be different. However, it is worth saying again among all the things we need to consider for revealing God's secrets, technologists and scientists need to consider the morality of the technology and its potential applications.

Inspiration Insights

1. Spending time with God rewires your brain and will give you more confidence in what He reveals to you.

2. Your work reputation is a critical credential in the marketplace. It can either give or take away your credibility.

3. Do not be intimidated by marketplace skepticism and criticism. Instead, use them to sharpen your skills of communicating your revelation into their culture and language.

4. While you develop a kernel of prophetic inspiration for work, make sure your revelation is relevant to your employer. Many good ideas are discarded because they are not relevant to the immediate problems your teammates face.

5. Evaluate the morality of the application of the revelation. I can personally assure you; you will not be the only one withholding revelation because you thought its application was immoral.

Translation and Communication

Vision is an essential element of the leader's job. But no vision is worth the paper it's printed on unless it is communicated constantly and reinforced with rewards.[15]

God wanted to move Israel from the wilderness to the Promised Land. Moses communicated that desire and stepped on the Promised Land's doorstep. Israel was nervous about laying hold of the promise and instead sent spies. Ten bad reports reinforced Israel's fears, and they turned around. What happened?

It is reasonable to say Moses failed to communicate the revelation in a way that was more compelling than Israel's fears. The same is true in the marketplace. If we fail to present revelation in a compelling way, the revelation will die before it is considered. We must transition our revelation to the language and culture of our marketplace.

---

[15] David Taylor, How Do Leaders Get Their Organizations From Vision to Action?, https://www.thinkingbusinessblog.com/2014/11/20/how-do-leaders-get-their-organizations-from-vision-to-action/, © 2014.

Marketplace Language

I had a compelling dream of the ISS solution. During my morning devotional, I became convinced my dream was a prophetic inspiration. On my bike ride to work, I had additional time to consider the relevance of the dream. When I arrived at work, I became even more convinced and started getting excited that God gave us the solution we needed.

But I made a big mistake that morning. I told my boss while walking to my office God gave me the solution in a dream. Why was that a mistake? Because my boss had no idea about how God works, prophecy, or divine dreams. He had no basis or foundation to understand or believe the information would be useful. In other words, he did not understand because I communicated in the language and culture of my church, not from a technical and scientific culture and point of view. He was not fluent in Christianese and therefore had no chance to understand my confidence. The evidence for my confidence was from my devotional and stemmed from my relationship with God. It is uniquely subjective. He needed objective evidence to be convinced. Fortunately, he asked me to explain.

Typically, our prophetic inspiration comes in visions, pictures, an inner certainty of truth, a word or phrase, or an equation; rarely is the inspiration complete, but it triggers a deeper understanding or conviction than the kernel of inspiration we receive. We generally cannot say to our workmates; I have a conviction from God my inspiration is going to work. We, therefore, need to communicate our prophetic inspiration to our peer groups, bosses, and companies' culture and language. That, for technologists, engineers, chemists, biologists and scientists, will likely be the language of science and technology, not dreams and visions.

My boss asked me to re-explain my dream and reminded me to explain my revelation in terms of my work culture. Until that time, I had not taken the time to understand the dream in my marketplace's culture and language. I shared with him what I remembered of the equation, explained how the computer program was going to modify the equation in many variables in an iterative process, and finally, how I intended to write a program to perform frequency-based statistical analysis on the data set the equations produced. I helped him understand that the vision of equations represented the performance of different parts in the communication system, and the solution was adding the respective systems parts equation models together as they represented the system. He asked if this had been done before. It had not been tried before. He had a lot of other detailed questions. Even though I had almost no answers, I valued his questions because they were the issues I needed to address in future communications. As we ended, he plainly said, "I don't know about God and how you talk with Him to get this stuff, but we have been working on this problem for more than nine months, and you are the first to offer any solution."

Notice there are two translations: First, inspired dreams, visions, images, and impressions… need to be translated into a communication infrastructure that uses a common understanding of the language and culture. Most Christians in technology and science will translate our revelations into our church's culture and language because that is where we received our introduction and training in receiving and communicating revelation. It is similar to people who speak multiple languages; they generally do math in the language they learn math even though they may live in a different culture for a long time. However, church language and culture are not very effective for communicating revelation in the marketplace. The revelation needs to be translated again. Once the second translation is made, the revelation can be effectively communicated in our marketplaces. In that sense, the marketplace prophet needs to be a language and culture translator.

You will be asked many questions by many people about your revelation. You accomplish two important and strategic objectives in communicating your revelation to your marketplace. First you validate your peers' and bosses' curiosity and interest and possibly build consensus and support. Second, you develop your skill of translating from your kernel of revelation to your marketplace culture and language skills.

Collaboration

During the Jesus-people revival, a little country church at the edge of town called Calvary Chapel in Costa Mesa, California, used to have 'afterglow' services after their Saturday and Sunday evening services. These were opportunities for people to develop their spiritual gifts like tongues, interpretation of tongues, healing the sick, vision and dreams, and the revelation gifts of words of wisdom, words of .knowledge, and prophecy. At any time, you could expect visions of butterflies and doves floating over the group, church, or city. People always read some scripture. Some spoke in tongues, and sometimes, they were interpreted. Nearly always, at least a couple of messages resonated with my spirit.

A common prophetic characteristic in the afterglow meetings was 'hopscotch' prophecy or revelation. Hopscotch prophecy is when one prophetic message triggers one or more additional messages. They all intertwined together to form a common and more complete theme. The best example is the Bible which spans over five thousand years and has a common theme throughout despite its multiple authors. This happens in the marketplace too. Your workmates may be holding ideas and revelations that are incomplete, and your revelation, sometimes incomplete, can be a prophetic catalyst for others. This collaboration is usually helpful.

Paul says we know in part and prophesy in part. (refer to 1 Corinthians 13:9). You cannot expect to catch all the nuances of your revelation and translate the revelation into language (sometimes twice) with complete proficiency. You should expect your team members to have partial or complete misunderstandings. Collaboration allows others to give you feedback on what they hear you saying. From there, you can further refine and elaborate the specifics of the revelation where people may need more information.

Many companies are finding research groups are more prolific in generating patents than an equivalent sum of individual researchers. Not surprisingly, the US Patent Office reports there are increasing numbers of patents having multiple inventors. Collaboration becomes the industry priority for science and technical development.

God's Grace

Do not miss that God's grace was all over my ISS experience, including my unsaved boss. All he knew about me is I was recommended to him by my technology colleagues. My boss and I worked together for only three or four months before I told him about my dream. I was an early career engineer while he was preparing for retirement, and I was the youngest in his group by at least a decade.

Having an inexperienced employee burst into his office first thing in the morning, before his cup of coffee and just after he hung up his sport jacket, must have been startling. It was the start of a habit for us that he eventually got used to. I blasted his sleepy mind saying I had a message from God. Even at his peak, he could not have understood what that meant. He was not a Christian and had no way to assess the value of divine revelation we have from the church. Had he had a church background, He would know about revelation and prophetic dreams and maybe had an internal experience that would tell him the revelation was indeed divine. He had none of that. God gave grace to him to ask me to explain again and allow him to be open to a solution that he often referred to as 'John's wild dream.' Do not underestimate the necessity for God's grace in every step of scientific and technical innovation. Not only is this a scientific process, but, importantly, this is a prayer journey needing a covering of God's grace.

Inspiration Insights

1. We need to compel our workmates by communicating our revelation convincingly above their skepticism and doubt.

This requires us to communicate in the marketplace's values and language without sacrificing the merit of the revelation.

2. Collaboration is of high value in the marketplace and is shown to advance technology. Accept feedback from and work with your teammates. Do not resist your workmates reshaping your communication, even to the point that it becomes very different than what you explained. This could very well be the process God intended. Try to remember you do not have the last word, God does.

3. Who does not need God's grace? Pray that your teammates will have the grace to see the revelation for what it is and that they are willing to collaborate on a journey of scientific and technical discovery and spirituality.

Development and Evolution

(Putting Flesh on Dry Bones)

"Opportunity is missed by most people because it is dressed in overalls and looks like work."

Thomas Edison

We like to think of scientific advancement in short timelines, but this is not the reality. In medicine, it takes an average of seventeen years for research evidence to reach clinical practice.[16] Even when I get an idea that will solve a problem on my hobby cars and work on it nearly daily, it can take a year or more to implement into a completed product.

Scientific historians talk about punctuated advancement. Revolutions occur when disparities or anomalies arise between theoretical expectations and research findings that can be resolved only by changing fundamental rules of practice. In a relative instant, the perceived relationships among the parts of

---

[16] Morris, Wooding, and Grant, "The answer is 17 years, what is the question: understanding time lags in translational research", Journal of the Royal Society of Medicine, 104(12), © 2011.
https://www.ncbi.nlm.nih.gov/pmc/articles/PMC3241518/#JRSM-11-0180C1

a picture shift, and the whole takes on a new meaning. Canonical examples include the Copernican idea that the Earth revolves around the Sun, relativity in physics, and the helical model of DNA.[17] Note the timeline of 'a relative instant' in all the examples took half a lifetime.

For scientific historians' typical scientific advancement occurs over many decades or millennia. The long evolutionary nature of scientific advancements, historians say, is due to the nature of breakthroughs, often being a convergence of enabling ideas from multiple disciplines.

Not every revelation will take a long time to develop into something that advances your program or technology. But then again, most of our revelations will not be like Einstein's theory of relativity. That said, when it comes to the process of getting a kernel of inspiration and the process to know it is worth pursuing, how much different is your revelation compared with Einstein's? James 5:17 might be relevant; "Elijah was a man with a nature like ours…" Elijah was arguably the greatest Old Testament prophet, and James says he is just like us. It was not Elijah that made him the greatest prophet, it was the revelation he received and delivered. Similarly, Einstein certainly had a high intellectual capacity to

---

[17] Feller I, Stern, A Strategy for Assessing Science: Behavioral and Social Research on Aging, National Academies Press (US); © 2007. https://www.ncbi.nlm.nih.gov/books/NBK26378/

develop revelation. However, the kernel of the inspiration for the theory of relativity was outside of who Einstein was as an intellect. Therefore, in terms of being prophetically inspired, we are just as likely to receive prophetic inspiration as Einstein. No matter what, all inspiration needs to be developed before it can have an impact on the marketplace and our communities.

The kernel of inspiration in my ISS dream had a series of equations overlaid across a graph showing real data and a trace outline similar to Figure , except the X variable was a random number that changed every second or so. There were six to eight images with different graph shapes floating in line with pluses between them. Every time the random numbers changed, a new set of slightly different graphs appeared. Before long, I was surrounded by these graphical equations with layers and layers of equations all around me. The last part of the dream was a zoom-out showing me in the middle of a sphere of hundreds or thousands of equation lines with a $\sum$ (the summation sign) to the left. When I woke after the dream, I wrote the equation on a notepad beside my bed and fell back to sleep.

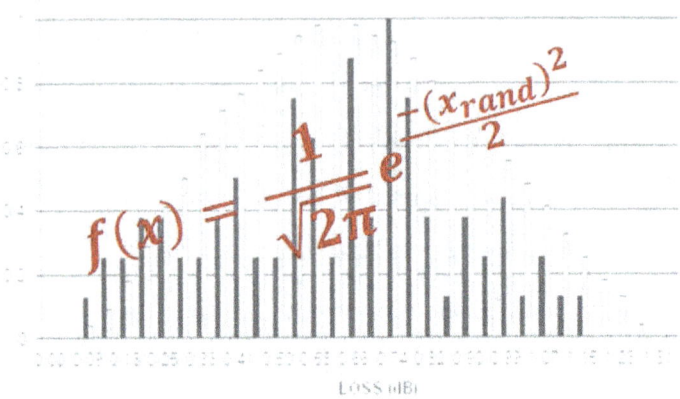

Figure 3 PDF equation

Forgive my tangent, but I recommend every technologist and scientist, and marketplace prophetic dreamer have a notepad beside their bed. You can jot down enough details about your dream, which will stimulate your memory in the morning. This can be script, drawings, names of people or places, a song, or a message related to a problem. When I was in a worship band, I kept a small recorder by my bed. I would record the lines and melodies I dreamed. Most of the time, you only need a little information to trigger your memory of the dream. Get in the habit of logging what you dream. A lot of times, you will find your dreams have little or no application. Sometimes, your dreams are divinely inspired and will save money, schedules, and programs. Additionally, a long log of dreams that have some conversions into the marketplace is a testimony of what God can do with a willing mind.

When I woke up the morning after the ISS dream, I looked at my notes and remembered all the details. However, I had no idea what it meant or why the Lord gave me the dream. During my morning devotional, a thought flashed through my mind that the dream was the solution to my problem at work. Until then, I had no idea because most dreams I have are not particularly relevant to me or are simply sorting through previous events. I spent the rest of my devotional time assessing if it was a dream from God and asking how it was the solution we were looking for.

At the time, the equation did not mean anything to me. I could not draw on my education or experience to validate the equations and algorithms in my dream. Specifically, I did not have the statistical mathematics background to know the significance of the equation; that it was an equation for a probability density function (PDF) shown in the background of Figure . By faith (which is the conviction of things not seen, reference Hebrews 11:1), I was convinced God gave me the solution to the ISS problem.

Being convinced you are prophetically inspired is one thing; having the faith to see prophetic inspiration through is another. 2 Corinthians 5:7 says, "… we walk by faith, not by sight." It is generally impossible to validate prophetic inspiration by what you know. Prophetic technologists must be convinced by faith to understand their prophetic dreams, visions, words, and equations... It is not that prophetic inspiration cannot be understood, in fact, it is your job to understand, communicate, and implement them. The prophetic inspiration you receive is generally only relevant to you, and it remains so until you communicate it to a specific recipient. There the conviction your prophetic revelation is from God requires a step of faith, not an act of science. This is what leads to the faith journey of disclosing your prophetic inspiration to others.

I already talked about my communication blunder with my boss. As I walked the thirty feet from my boss's office to mine, I became overwhelmed by the task that lay ahead and by the commitment I had just made; a solution in six months seemed impossible. I just convinced my boss to commit six months plus other company resources based on a dream I did not understand and could not clearly explain. When I got to my desk, I asked myself what I had done and started praying that infamous prayer of humanity, "Oh God, oh God, oh God!" I didn't know where to start, let alone how to create a solution. In just those short thirty feet, I saw Peter's waves of doubt before me. I began to sink into the despair of the impossible task ahead and had to call out to Jesus to save me. I had nothing else.

Two things are noteworthy; first, trying to use what you learned to validate prophetic inspiration is like trying to use your shoe as a spatula for flipping your morning omelet. Your education and experiences are the tools that can develop your kernel of inspiration into marketplace language, but they are incapable of convincing you of the merit of a prophetic inspiration because they do not operate in the same domain. Secondly, people having a relationship with God can ask if a revelation originated with Him. I am convinced that when God gives a prophetic inspiration, He is also interested in seeing through, even if that means your company or peers are not convinced. Christian technologists have a huge advantage in scientific discovery and advancement because they are immersed in a church community where revelation gifts are commonly learned, developed, used, and shared. These tools translate well to the marketplace.

Developing marketplace prophetic inspiration is different than 'giving a word' in church. In church, the person receiving the inspiration does the specific development of the revelation. Our church culture has taught us the receiver is responsible for seeing if the message is from God, verifying the message is relevant for them, and finally, the receiver is responsible for implementing the message into something that brings about change for good. In the marketplace, the inspired person generally introduces their revelation to their team, which often starts a collaborative effort to determine its relevance to their team. If the team is convinced, they may pursue developing the revelation into advances in scientific understandings, methods of solving problems, and technologies that change products or give a competitive advantage. Some of your revelations will be developed by someone else or another group altogether.

When you have the chance to lead the development, start by telling a small group; one or two Christian technologists would be ideal. Doing so takes some burden off translating your revelation into the marketplace language and culture. Your spiritually sensitive friends can help create the narrative needed when collaborating with larger marketplace groups to your non-Christian technologist colleagues and bosses.

I was fortunate when I worked on the ISS program; I had a Christian workmate and friend who was a brilliant mathematician. I told him about my dream and showed him the equation. He instantly recognized the equation as a PDF equation, and he identified the multiple equations that continued to iterate with random numbers as a Monte Carlo statistical analysis. A Monte Carlo analysis is like rolling dice many times and logging the number each roll shows. Statistical analysis is generally performed on the resulting data set. I asked him to teach me more, but he said he had a college book at home, and everything I needed to know was in chapters 6, 8, and 9. Not only was he a brilliant mathematician, but his memory is unmatched by anyone I know. These two attributes made him invaluable in performing his job of approving flight computer code and made him particularly helpful later in the development of the Monte Carlo computer algorithm. The next morning, I found the book on my desk.

In about two or three weeks, I learned the math I needed, I knew the proper terms, and I was able to communicate my dream in correct mathematical terms with my peers. With my brief explanation, the NASA team wanted to 'approve' the project but asked for a detailed presentation. The presentation explained how I intended to:

1. Measure the stressed and unstressed performance of each of the critical parts of the communication link. For each data set, I would plot a probability density function (PDF).

2. Create mathematical models having the same PDF as the data. The equations would be based on random number generators that would give a wide distribution within the bounds of the data's PDF. These models were effectively the dice that generated the Monte Carlo data.

3. To simulate the system, I added the representative models in the same order as the design configuration of the communication system, with each model having its own random number generator. One model for each part.

4. To create an MS Excel macro (program) that summed the results of each calculation iteration and performed a basic statistical analysis of the data set created by iterating the summation of the model in the system configurations.

5. Give the outputs in probability density and cumulative distribution plots with a marker showing performance at the 99.7% confidence level.

Of the approximately twenty-five people viewing the presentation, only three or four were interested and offered help. They all had PhDs which comforted me since I was venturing into an unknown area and thought they would have many great contributions. In the end, their contributions were limited to validating the approach, which was crucial for NASA to approve and support the project.

To make the component performance models, I built fifteen samples of six different parts and measured their stressed and non-stressed performance. I then graphed the data as a PDF for that given component and stress condition. I created equations composed of exponential, logarithmic, and linear random number functions. I bound the equations by the performance limits of the part data sets. Lastly, I created a random number generator equation whose PDF matched the data set of each of the components' PDFs. For each system containing any combination of the six stress or unstressed parts, I simply added the random number equation generator for each component model. Each iteration of random numbers gave a unique overall system performance value. I used a macro I wrote in MS Excel to perform the statistical functions to calculate the mean and standard deviation of the data set. I created an Excel macro to calculate the student's T and chi-square approximation for the variable confidence interval and created a method of plotting the PDF and CDF (Cumulative Distribution Function) system model results.

An 80386 processor PC was available to me, and it had the latest copy of Microsoft Excel v2 on it. While I was familiar with assembly, Basic, and FORTRAN programming languages from school, I wanted to learn Excel, and this seemed like a good opportunity. But the challenge was MSExcel v2 did not have the statistical package I needed.

After four or five months, I integrated all my models, the MS Excel macros, and my plotting worksheets and set out to run the first calculation. I hit the F9 button that starts an MSExcel calculation which was the default in those days. I waited for a couple of seconds. Oh No! The blue screen of death! The algorithm was simply too large for the 80386 without a math coprocessor to handle. I needed a better computer with a math coprocessor. A colleague had just received an 80486 processor personal computer. I was able to borrow it at night. That computer was able to run the complete program in about eight or nine hours on small ISS communication system simulations. When calculating the performance of the larger systems, the 80486 computer crashed or gave bad data about half the time, which undermined our confidence in all the results.

Fortunately, Intel released its Pentium processor, and my company ordered its first Pentium computer for me. Pentium computers not only had a bigger and faster processor but also had an integrated math coprocessor that was much more capable than the previous add-on math coprocessors available for the 80386 and 80486 personal computers. The Pentium computer ran the small systems in a few seconds and on large systems in less than five minutes using the same MS Excel V.2 software.

Because it took two months to order and receive the Pentium computer, the full development cycle, from prophetic dreams to printed solutions, took a total of eight months. Even though everything seemed to work as intended, and I asked several brilliant people to verify the math, there were still skeptics asking how accurately the predictions represented real systems. I will tell you more about that later.

Inspiration insights

1. Converting prophetic inspiration is long, hard, tedious work.

2. Scientific breakthrough often occurs as a result of many enabling (and seemingly indirect) events.

3. Your unsaved workmates will not gain confidence in knowing God gave you an idea. They are going to use the tools and experience they know to judge the merit of your revelation. So, we need to communicate our revelation in their language.

4. Collaborating with Christian technologists can help you develop a marketplace understanding and language to share your ideas with a broader audience.

5. Expect roadblocks along the way. Who would have expected the solution that I developed from a dream would also need a new computer that was not being sold at the time I had the dream? The solution could not be fully realized until I could run the program on a Pentium computer.

There are always skeptics. Some of them might not know the project was initiated with a prophetic revelation. Look for opportunities to improve when considering what they address.

Qualification and Verification

How do you qualify and verify a dream? A common difficulty of advancing technology is qualifying it. Einstein needed to develop new math to prove relativity. Throughout the TV show 'The Big Bang,' Sheldon Cooper is shown trying to develop math for his version of String Theory. Sheldon's work was modeled after Brian Greene's work, who is a leading proponent of String Theory.

I worked for about six months on integrating the statistical analysis package into Excel and another month creating data models for the stressed and unstressed parts, which created encouraging results; there were no preexisting models or data that could validate the outputs. Therefore, the validation needed to come from analysis but outside of the tools I developed. I needed to return to my math friend whose job was qualifying flight computer codes.

I asked him to review and validate the equations that formed the data models and to review the math in the MS Excel macros. A couple of days later, to my dismay but not unsurprising, he showed me several equation limits errors that needed attention. After reworking the equation models, worksheets, and macros to his satisfaction, it was time to present my analysis tool, procedures, and simulation results to the larger ISS team.

I presented my math, the block diagram of how I thought I programmed Excel and my results. NASA asked for the Excel workbook and presentation for evaluation. It was hard to hand it over because I knew it would be critically scrutinized. NASA's immediate feedback was the program was unstable because their computers were crashing, something I told them might happen. When I realized they were going to take two or three weeks to review everything, I decided to go one step further in the qualification. I built some prototypes of the large ISS data and communication systems. I developed an experimental method that allowed me to stress selected parts in the system. It also made the prototype systems easily reconfigurable to create similar systems but with specific parts in different sequences. That allowed me to create another PDF of the large systems in different configurations and compare the data PDFs with the MS Excel analysis results. As it turned out, the calculated data was about 10% or 15% more conservative than the measured data, but in general, the data I collected of thirty-five different system configurations and the analysis tool were very close.

I shared my results with the ISS team at about the same time they reported they were satisfied with the basic concept and tool. They had some suggestions, but most were related to the outputs of the analysis tool. They also shared they used it to qualify another program with 'favorable' results. After their analysis, coupled with the new data I presented, NASA approved the analysis tool and its results.

This is what is currently happening in the global climate change industry. Global climate change models still have not been proven. Models from the 1960s through the 1970s predict a cooling trend. Michael Mann, Raymond Bradley, and Malcolm Hughes used new statistical methods in their MBH98 and MHG99 climate models, otherwise known as the hockey stick models, which remain unproven at the time of this writing. The obvious dilemma is the long-forecast climate model has not been around long enough to see significant forecasts and then measure a temperature change in the future. California University at Berkeley and NASA researchers at the Goddard Institute of Space Studies decided to review recorded history. They used temperature data from 1970 to 2007 in the analysis tools to predict temperatures from 2007 to 2017 (also historical data). In 2020, the research was approved for publication, indicating no evidence that the climate models evaluated either systematically overestimated or underestimated warming over the period of their projections.[18] However, the article says the ten older climate models they evaluated needed compensation for *'carbon dioxide and other uncertainties.'*

NASA's approach to proving climate prediction models, just like my experience proving my models and analysis tools, was data-driven, using a subset of data to predict the next, or in my example, the worst case, performance interval.

<u>Inspiration Insights</u>

1. Proving prophetic inspiration in the marketplace relies on the same skills, tools, and experience gained in school through your experience in the marketplace. Generally, the proof and validation will be an application of the scientific method.

2. Even a highly skilled group might not be able to prove a prophetic revelation. Collaboration is common and broadens the experience base. The proof of the entire development might boil down to verifying one part of what has been developed at a time.

---

[18] Alan Buis, "Study Confirms Climate Models are Getting Future Warning Projections Right", © 2020, https://climate.nasa.gov/news/2943/study-confirms-climate-models-are-getting-future-warming-projections-right/

Implementation

Developing prophetic inspiration to the point of implementation typically takes a long time. In my example, I received prophetic inspiration more than five years before the International Space Station elements were launched and the astronauts started building the communication system in space. In today's fast-paced work environment, many employees do not stay at their companies that long. In 2022, the average tenure for software developers and engineers is only four and a half years[19]. This means technologists may leave their positions and programs before their prophetic revelations come to fruition. This can create anxiety about future creative activities, and somehow, technologists fear they will not be as effectively creative at their next assignment. However, I haven't witnessed anyone's creativity diminish by changing companies.

For the most part, prophetic people in the Bible are consistently prophetic. There are cases like Saul during his induction into his position as king over Israel, where he prophesied for short periods. Afterward, there are no additional mentions of his prophetic activities. This could be

---

[19] Smith, "How Long Do Software Engineers Stay at a Job?" DevelopperPitstop.com, © 2021.

because the story's theme is about Saul becoming king, not about him being a prophet. However, taken at face value, it is important to note that Saul prophesied when 'the Spirit came on him' (1 Samuel 10:10). In the same way, God will grace us with divine inspiration. But this is only one small way that we receive divine revelation.

Our confidence today is that Jesus promised the Holy Spirit would continually abide with believers. Therefore, our primary ability to receive prophetic inspiration and revelation does not come and go as it did with Saul. On the contrary, we are assured the Holy Spirit remains in us, and His presence rests upon us as we practice the disciplines of hosting His presence. Therefore, revelation becomes common in the lives of believers, even when it is recognized.

Typically, new product development technologists do not see their prophetic revelations mature through manufacturing in large companies. Companies generally want their researchers to focus on new product development rather than manufacturing. But do not think that prophetic revelation is limited to research. Spirit-led process and manufacturing engineers are no less able to receive prophetically inspired ideas and revelations. When they do, the development and implementation of their prophetic inspiration can enable new products to be realized and save their companies manufacturing costs by streamlining the manufacturing processes and improving the quality of the product. In fact, this focus on improving manufacturing efficiency and product quality is exactly what W. Edwards Deming championed in the 1970s. He called it Total Quality Management (TQM), and it propelled Japanese automakers from producing undesirable, inexpensive cars to becoming the automotive superpower it is today.

The role of technologists in small companies is much different than my ISS experience. Small companies rely on their technologist to guide the technology from its inception in product development through manufacturing or what is commonly called 'from womb to tomb' development. This includes all development of new ideas, the unveiling of new technology and possible product introductions, qualification and verification, and manufacturing support throughout the product's lifetime.

Our experience with prophetic inspiration in the church is that most revelations find their home and produce the results our Healer and Comforter intends. Therefore, you might think all marketplace revelation is easily implemented because it originates with the Creator. But unfortunately, this is not the case. In aerospace, internal and government-funded research rarely translates to the production of novel products, even when patents are issued. Only ten to fifteen percent of research transitions into production.

While I have used the example of the successful revelation and implementation of an analysis tool for the ISS data and communication system, the reality is that I have many prophetic revelations that did not make the cut. Of those, some were patented, others were declared competition sensitive but not patented, and a few did not progress any further than a conversation with my peers. Others were rejected by my team and/or my organization.

Sometimes, timing or organizational priorities are not aligned with the processes of developing prophetic solutions. This can be disappointing to technologists, especially when they know their ideas are heaven-sent. Discouragement often comes when your prophetic inspiration is rejected or disregarded. You might think you have lost your ability to receive the kernels of prophetic inspiration because no one seems interested. That is not true.

As we have been discussing, there are many skills required to see marketplace revelation mature to production that has nothing to do with your spirituality. Like me, you might need to learn how to communicate spiritual ideas in the marketplace language. You might need to develop your analytical skills. These are skills you can learn and develop and have nothing to do with your spirituality. As a prophetic technologist in the marketplace, don't blame or undermine your spirituality when your inspiration does not move forward at your workplace.

A friend of mine fell off a horse and sustained paralyzing injuries. When he was in the hospital, I received a word that God would heal him within two weeks. The doctors continued the prescribed medical interventions for his condition, which included multiple surgeries within that same two weeks. They said the surgeries were necessary for him live beyond the hospital. In my mind, some of the surgeries could have interfered with his health if God were to miraculously heal him. By two weeks, he had four surgeries, and it looked like the opportunity for healing slowly diminished to the point that it seemed impossible, at least the way I imagined it.

Not seeing my friend healed after receiving a clear word about his healing caused me to doubt my ability to hear God and my prophetic instincts. It is thirty years later and it remains one of my biggest disappointments. However, I did not let it shape me or my prophetic theology or practice. I still believe God speaks. I still believe I hear God's voice. I still believe God wants me to share my prophetic insight. At the same time, I still believe there is room to improve and grow. It is important to maintain a biblically based theology rather than an experience-based theology, especially in the midst of a disappointing outcome of the exercise of your faith.

What do you do when your friend doesn't receive the healing you expected by prophetic revelation or you don't get traction on your prophetic revelation at your workplace? You keep being faithful to giving words of divine revelation for healing, for well-being, and for scientific advancement.

Similarly, prophetic revelation in the marketplace that does not get developed can be difficult for the marketplace prophet. Your conviction about your revelation helping your project and organization never dies, but without the support from your organization, the revelation is just fruit hanging on the tree. When that happens, we need to let our organizations' decisions prevail, even if it is at their own cost. Importantly, their decision is not a reflection on your ability to obtain prophetic inspiration.

Having led research and development groups throughout my career, I witnessed many successful R&D technologists transfer to production departments. They say they want to work on something 'important' enough to be in production. These transfers sometimes reflect the researcher's personal offense when their new technology is not developed. If we limit our responsibility to sharing the revelation and allow the approving people, group, or organization to be responsible for taking the next step, we can avoid this disappointment. In this case, our evaluation of the prophetic inspiration is based on our communication with our teammates.

Here is some encouragement. Firstly, and worth repeating, realize your peers' or organizations' approval and support do not determine the quality of your revelation nor the character, quality, and efficacy of your spiritual life. There are many factors involved, and none of them reflects directly on how God inspires and loves you. Unimplemented prophetic revelation does not mean God is displeased with you or you got it wrong. Many times, it may be contingent on your peers' or organizations' decision not to pursue the revelation.

Secondly, like giving words at church, your capacity to receive future revelation grows by giving the revelations you get. The converse is true; you lose the skill and capacity to gain revelation if you are not in the habit of seeking and sharing revelation. God is a good investor; He deposits His treasures in people who wisely and successfully invest what He entrusts to them. A prophet's responsibility is to give revelation, not to realize the revelation to a specific outcome.

Lastly, it is wise for a marketplace prophet to stay in a supportive prophetic community. For most of us, that supportive prophetic community will be our church. Even if your prophetic community is not targeting the marketplace, you will find others' stories of how they received and processed their kernels of inspiration helpful, encouraging, and reaffirming. Being in a prophetic community is more important than reading a good book on prophecy, even this book. As the saying goes, 'Spiritual things are easier caught than taught.'

Let's end this section by talking about the glory of implementation. Since the ISS was launched and assembled in orbit, I am proud when I see the videos on board the station knowing the systems I developed are still working. Seeing it fly across the sky is the validation of my prophetic dream was the kernel of inspiration that created an analysis that was later used on many other aerospace platforms. These parts of the communication systems are now commodities and rarely are scrutinized and analyzed like they were on the ISS. But this is the inevitable end for the technology we develop, and the technologies must move on.

It is a wonder and praise when prophetic inspiration and revelation are developed in the marketplace. Your colleagues and organization will soon recognize your contributions (reference Proverbs 18:16). Because of your testimony, God gets the glory for solving problems or creating new projects and products no one else could.

Inspiration Insights

1. Be tenacious and patient while developing your prophetic inspiration into an actionable concept, process, or product. You will likely be the cheerleader for the revelation through a process that can take years to complete.

2. Do not get discouraged and disappointed when your teammates, bosses, and companies do not authorize the development of your last prophetic inspiration to keep you from seeking a new one.

3. Give God glory when you see your prophetic inspiration realized.

Tell the World

Time differentiates prophecy from history.

When I was first married, I received a word about my wife. I was learning how to receive and process prophetic words, and I was excited to tell her what I had learned. After telling her, I expected her to say, "Wow, that was really helpful and gives me great insight." That was not how she responded! Let's just say the word was not received well. What happened? Did I get the revelation wrong? No, I did not understand one of the responsibilities of a prophetic person.

Not every prophetic revelation is intended to be revealed, or at least not when it is received. This insight about my wife was given to me so I could understand what the Holy Spirit was doing in my wife so I could, in turn, support and encourage her through the process and that season. The revelation was about my wife, not for my wife.

Prophetic inspiration in the marketplace can be similarly time bound to the events and culture within your workplace. Some revelations turn into patents. Most technology companies reward patenting ideas with monetary incentives, and some companies will share royalties and licensing income. But getting a patent does not mean the revelation was timely.

When patents are issued too early, the inventor(s) and patent awardee(s) get little benefit because the patent expires before the marketplace needs the technology. In these cases, the chances for royalties and licensing are forfeited. It is more profitable to employers when the inventor waits until the marketplace is ready for the revelation and innovation. We need to keep an eye on our marketplace and be sensitive to the timing of releasing new technology.

I recently had a dream of a solution for a problem my organization did not know was about to have. I knew right away; God gave revelation to me in a dream. That night through the morning, I developed the idea and made a PowerPoint presentation explaining the problem they do not have yet, but likely will. The next day, I presented the details of the problem and solution it to my teammates and boss. I explained the issues we would have and how the revealed solution would consistently solve the problem with little impact on our production and a low cost. At the end of the meeting, my boss asked why we were trying to solve a problem we did not have. I explained the solution's hardware would take time to develop and manufacture; if we wait, our options will be limited to a lesser elegant solution that will have production impacts and whose correct implementation could not be verified. He decided to wait. As I write this, I am trying to refine the less desirable, more difficult-to-implement solution I warned my team about.

Just like giving words in church, some are accepted, and some are rejected no matter how right and accurate they are; the same is true in the marketplace. The difference is, in church, people know to evaluate a revelation to see if it applies to them or their circumstances. In the marketplace, your word will be evaluated by your teammates and bosses. A technology group decides your revelation's technical and business merits. Further, when you give revelation in the marketplace, you or your team will champion the revelation throughout your organization and sometimes into white papers, technology conferences, peer-reviewed papers, and magazine articles. While presenting a revelation to broader technology groups and to the public can be daunting, it also opens the door to show the technology world how a relationship with God can significantly change their world.

Most leading-edge technologists and scientists work in secure buildings with limited access making us the only people in our church community carrying God's presence, reality, and revelation to our teammates, bosses, and marketplace collaborators. Most pastors freely acknowledge they know nothing about my work culture and, importantly, its language and priorities. Their access to non-Christians in the technology marketplace is limited. God placed Christians like you and me in these places to bring His Kingdom to our workmates and our specialty fields.

Get used to the idea; you will repeatedly communicate your developed prophetic inspiration and the technical justification for the specific application many times. You will likely not only be the primary advocate, but sometimes you need to be a cheerleader for the implementation of your developed prophetic inspiration. But this is also an opportunity to share with your colleagues how you were inspired.

My early research work gave me many opportunities to lecture at technology conferences. My company had a policy requiring company approval for lectures, articles, and white papers. So early in my experience as a conference lecturer and technical paper author, I would present my company's advancements by rigorously following my company's approved information. The audience often did not ask many technical questions outside the company's boundaries.

After years of presenting and as people were more familiar with my company's accomplishments, their questions started changing. Instead of being limited to technical questions, they began asking about what I thought was the reason my company had so many new things to talk about year after year. I typically said I was grateful to work at a company that allows and values research and development and that I found my teammates to be unusually inspired.

It seemed I often ran out of time answering questions. To make sure everyone received the answers they deserved, I made myself available after the lectures. This was sometimes in an unused room but mostly in the hallways outside the lecture hall. By far, the most common follow-on question asked was how people are inspired and what was the development process for inspiration. I would talk about how God gave me dreams and speaks to me in prayer.

Some of the audience that gathered walked away when I started talking about divine inspiration; most stayed. I know some critics asked the conference organizers to bar spiritual conversations. In an attempt to appease the critics, some organizers asked me to refrain from mentioning God in my lectures. I pointed out I followed my company-approved lecture notes which were sent months earlier, and the lectures did not have spiritual content. The conference organizers then focused on the questions and answers sections. Responding I asked, "What is more useful to advance technology in our field, saying I am the sole source of all my revelation and thereby privatizing technology advancement, or saying God is the source of my technology advancement and He can inspire others too?" Only one conference organizer group asked me to stop talking about God's revelation after the lectures.

Our marketplace colleagues are starving for inspiration, especially those working in research and development. We have an open door to their mind, hearts, and soul by telling how God inspires us. In a nutshell, this is our world of evangelism.

Someone may say, "I am not good at apologetics and convincing others to start a relationship with Jesus." Many pastors tell us, while many technologists and scientists cringe, Matthew 25 tells us to evangelize the world. They say this means having spiritual conversations with others at work. We know telling our workmates about Christ is difficult because of the environment of unbelief and because, in many workplaces, having spiritual conversations is grounds for workplace discipline. One of my workmates reported me for praying for someone's healing in my office. I answered HR asking if it is better to let someone suffer without hope of relief or better to pray with the hope they will get better and in some cases do feel better. In the end, HR asked me to pray in more private places.

Before Mathew tells us to preach the gospel, Mathew tells us to go into the world and make disciples. Many Christians understand Matthew's imperative as a charge to save the world and our workmates because we have been taught the discipleship process starts with salvation. But does it? Suppose discipleship can happen before conversion. If this is possible, waiting for a salvation decision impedes disciple-making. I do not think there is a Godly mandate to save a soul before disciplining the person.

Accepting Christ is not easy. A person must come to the point where they are willing to abandon their entire life and live under Christ's paradigm and rule. As far as I understand, this is the only 'stumbling block' Jesus allows. Joel Barker, a brilliant management and organization thinker, says, "When [one] paradigm shifts, everything goes to zero."[20] Most of our workmates have systematically chosen their life pathways, and the thought of giving it all up for a faith commitment can be rejected simply on the basis that they have methodically planned and invested in their current lives. This is on top of their many objections to religion, Christianity, and sometimes to Jesus.

Unfortunately, we rarely have the time or opportunity to unpack misconceptions in an apology to our workmates. Not many times do we have an opportunity to discuss the many benefits of Christianity. Therefore, if we wait until conversion

---

[20] Joel Barker, "Paradigms: The Business of Discovering the Future," Harper Business, © 1993.

before we start disciplining our workmates, we may forfeit all evangelistic opportunities altogether.

A perfect example of Christian discipling before salvation is exemplified in the right-to-life movement. This movement has been making disciples of Jesus without requiring their salvation for a long time. Their evangelistic model starts by appealing to people's sense of morality. The right-to-life movement starts discipling by giving their unsaved supporters tools that support their moral positions, but they show where these moral positions are supported biblically and scientifically. Many unsaved people joining the right-to-life movement eventually gave their hearts to Jesus. For them, discipleship occurred before they accepted Christ into their lives.

Like the right-to-life movement, we should seize every opportunity to disciple a coworker, remembering salvation is not a prerequisite. In the technology marketplace, discipling can be started by helping people understand their dreams and impression in the Christian context that God is speaking to them.

I start prophetic inspiration discipleship by encouraging technologists to dream big. Often my teammates' ideas are undeveloped dreams or visions that look more like prophetic inspiration than a scientific recipe. Unfortunately, they lack the tools to convert their inspiration to a scientific hypothesis. I will ask them questions about the small details of their inspiration for the idea. Most technical people distrust their non-verbal intuition. By guiding colleagues to elaborate on the details of their inspiration, we sometimes see novel and important concepts, visions, and ideas. Once there are sufficient details, we can start to formalize their ideas into the marketplace language and culture, start the technology development and, when applicable, write a patent disclosure, write a white paper, or offer a revelation as a solution to advance their project. This is very rewarding for the technologist.

These conversations are useful in other ways. First, I learn about how my colleague thinks and how inspiration comes to them. I also learn how they communicate non-technical information. Learning how inspiration comes to them and how they think in non-technical terms allows us to communicate our prophetic inspiration in their native intuitive and inventive language. We also earn their trust with things that go beyond their education and job responsibilities which opens the doors to meaningful spiritual conversation.

I have assisted more people in developing their vague ideas resulting in more patents than I have personally received. More importantly, while teaching them how to press into inspiration, how to convert inspiration to marketplace language, develop their ideas into a marketplace reality, and champion their ideas at their workplaces, I developed a relationship that creates an evangelistic bridge without taking the time for an apologetic argument. Through the discipleship of unpacking revelation, they experience what it means to be heavenly gifted, which draws them to the gift giver.

Inspiration Insights

1. There are many considerations when revealing your prophetic inspiration. Is it the right time? Is my revelation relevant to my organization? Will my revelation be used morally?

2. Most technologists and scientists have access to nonbelieving coworkers our church leadership will never have. We are in the best position to bring the light of Christ to our coworkers.

3. Technologists and scientists are starving for inspiration. We have a story they want to hear, even if it conflicts with their spiritual priorities.

4. We can disciple coworkers by helping them understand their intuitive ideas. This opens the door to explaining that God gives the ideas and is pleased they are pursuing them. For some, this could be the first time they experience God's pleasure.

5. It is common that what you develop will take you to new places and put you in new situations far outside your workplace. It can take on a life of its own. It could even lead to a change in career paths.

Remembrance and Memorials

This Space Shuttle launch picture is taken by NASA at 3:35 A.M, 4 December 1998, from five miles away. That morning, the Space Shuttle carried the first US element, Node 1, of the International Space Station. After seeing the Space Shuttle clear the tower, roll, and start heading down range, you hear the engines roar and feel the noise in your chest. Because it was at night and from my viewing position, I was able to see the separation of the solid rocket boosters and the main engines burn for about three minutes after separation. It was the first time I watched a Space Shuttle launch in person, and I was absolutely amazed. But none of the spectacle I experienced compared to the pride I felt. This picture memorializes the years of development, manufacturing, testing, and validation, sleepless nights, many trips from California to Houston and

Florida, working with a lot of great and super talented people and meeting some really tough deadlines. It is in a photo roll I use as my screen saver at work and sometimes at home.

God gave instructions to Israel about keeping the Sabbath. One of the instructions was to remember their history with God. Sometimes, to ensure Israel would remember God's mighty works, God instructed Israel to build memorials. One of those times was immediately after crossing the Jordon; God told Jacob to stack stones out of the river as a memorial. God specifically instructs them, "Tell your children what God has done for you today."

Reflecting on the successes of your prophetic inspiration is a technologist's spiritual discipline, just like Israel's memorials. My desk is cluttered with memorials, not twelve big stones, but some of the things developed from God's whisperings to me. When people ask, I have an opportunity to tell how I had a dream; I saw a solution in a daydream or picture that flashed before my eyes when I was looking for a design. Thirty years ago, unsaved technologists sneered at my stories about God's inspiration for a design or invention. However, the technology marketplace culture changed, and people are more open to spiritual conversations, and some technologists are starving for it.

When I left the Space Station program, my retired boss toasted me at my farewell party. He told the story of how ten years prior, a young engineer who had just joined his group burst into his office early one morning, saying, "God gave me the solution to a problem that stumped some of the smartest people he knew." He said he didn't know what to make of the 'crazy kid,' but one thing he learned over time was that if I said I felt I had a solution from God, the best thing he could do was let me go try because it usually led to amazing results. He concluded his toast by saying, "I don't know if there is a God or not, but if there is one, John seems to know Him, and his God is a very good source of John's engineering inspiration."

The memorials we make could be trinkets on our desks or remembering a nice speech from your boss. However, I think the important memorial is our workmate's witness of the prophetic inspiration they see in you and me.

Finale

We live in a world of scientific wonder and mystery. A common saying, "We don't know what we don't know," is certainly true. But that is not to say the scientific community does not know anything about what they do not know. The Higgs' Boson, formally called 'the God particle,' is the particle that is associated with quantum fields. It is yet to be proven. Similarly, we understand eighty percent of the universe is made of 'dark matter,' but we do not know what dark matter is exactly. There seems to be no shortage of things to be discovered, spanning the subatomic to astronomic fields. It seems there is a divine plan for scientific discovery: God gave humans curiosity and an insatiable drive to understand their world, and, at the same time, God created a world whose rules and laws are observable and measurable.

These unending unanswered scientific questions give us incredible opportunities to advance science and technology by receiving prophetic revelation, translating them into the language of our scientific culture, and using the skills and experiences to prove and apply what we perceive as the kernel of inspiration.

By telling my story about a dream that solved a major problem on the ISS, I gave an example of how to process a dream into an application that helped my project and company. I discussed my mistakes and made some recommendations to help you introduce prophetic inspiration at your workplace. Without a doubt, the way you receive prophetic revelation, the way you process revelation, your church and marketplace cultures, and your education and experiences will have more influence over the way you present prophetic inspiration to your workplace community than this book.

You might ask, "Can every technologist get prophetic downloads?" The Bible is clear on the fact that not everyone has a 'gift of prophecy,' but, as we know, you do not need the 'gift of prophecy' to give a prophetic word. Therefore, it is possible God may call on you to advance your project or company through divine inspiration.

Some Christian cynics might say, "Why is God interested in science and technology?" I can think of several reasons. First, we agree that God's fingerprints are all over creation. Discoveries overwhelmingly seem to reveal God's glory, not take away from it. Second, God delights when His children are promoted. Scientists and technical people are promoted when they are successful and inspiration adds to their success. Third, God's gets the glory when a Christian technologist says how he came across a novel idea, process, method, or application. Fourth, in a marketplace starved for innovation and spiritual transformation, the Christian technologist's testimony has a bigger impact. We can have a part of not only changing our marketplace but also bridging the gap between science and faith. Lastly, in line with Larry Norman's famous question:

Why should the devil have all the good inventions?

The End

About the Author

John White worked in aerospace research and development for more than forty years. Among his accomplishments are patents, accommodations from NASA, SAE, IEEE, and his employers. He has mentored many engineers, technologists, and scientists, as well as teaching college Physics.

John also received a BA from Vanguard University in Religion, Ministry, and Leadership. Since 2000 when he met Christ, he has been involved in worship, discipleship, and spiritual formation. He led a traveling worship band in the late 1980s and has held leadership positions as a small group ministry director, church elder, and board member.

Married since 1983, his growing family with a lovely and wise wife, two successful kids, and a growing number of grandkids is an everyday blessing.

Acknowledgements

Had it not been for the Bethel's leadership team's suggestion to write my story, this book would never have existed. Bill, Kris and Ryan thank you for your nudges and support.

Bill Dogterom, my professor at Vanguard University, who was one of the first people that recognized my approach to science and technology and theology was worth exploring and developing. I appreciate the academic freedom to explore and mature many subjects.

Lastly, I owe Robin Gough and Lisa J my loving gratitude for the many hours they spent reviewing and commenting on my manuscript. Their fingerprints are all over this.

www.ingramcontent.com/pod-product-compliance
Lightning Source LLC
LaVergne TN
LVHW020134080526
838202LV00047B/3937